C

Interview Q&A

(Guide to crack Software Companies' Interviews)

Second Edition

C

Interview Q&A

(Guide to crack Software Companies' Interviews)

Second Edition

Sandeep A. Thorat

MTech Computer Science (IIIT Hyderabad)

SHROFF PUBLISHERS & DISTRIBUTORS PVT. LTD.

Mumbai *Bangalore* *Kolkata* *NewDelhi*

C Interview Q & A, Second Edition

by Sandeep A. Thorat

First Edition: July 2011

Second Edition: October 2012

ISBN 13: 978-93-5023-817-2

Published by **Shroff Publishers & Distributors Pvt. Ltd.** C-103, T.T.C. Industrial Area, M.I.D.C., Pawane, Navi Mumbai - 400 705. Tel.: (91-22) 4158 4158 Fax: (91-22) 4158 4141 E-mail: spdordersshroffpublishers.com. Printed at Decora Book Prints Pvt. Ltd., Mumbai.

Dedicated To

My beloved Father and Mother
For their everlasting Love, Care and Support.

Preface

A Book on

"C Interview Q&A"

C language is one of most fundamental programming technique & has a huge importance in software industries. Almost all software companies conduct technical Aptitude Tests based on C language in their recruitment process. C Language questions are frequently asked in technical interviews as well. The proficiency in C Language is important to crack GATE Computer Science examination.

C language is part of syllabus of various engineering disciplines, BCA, MCA and MSc(Computer Science) curriculums. Due to academic curriculum students became familiar with C, but very few of them have command over C language. The questions asked in recruitment process are tricky & tests C syntax, logical, analytical & debugging abilities of the students. By keeping these things in our mind, we are proposing a book which covers almost all different types of objective questions asked on C Language. We have also given explanation of each answer; this is useful to students for understanding concepts. All questions discussed in the book are tested in MD-DOS Turbo C environment and utmost care is taken to give precise answers.

The proposed book would be useful for students of different engineering branches who are willing to do their carrier in Software Industries. The book is also useful to MCA, BSc & MSc(Computer Science) and MCS students. Also book would be quite useful to crack GATE Computer Science examination.

Key Features of the Book are -:

1. The answers of each objective question are explained.
2. The Questions focus is on making conceptual understanding and not syntax.
3. Sufficient number of examples given to cover different aspects.
4. All programs and answers in the Book are tested on standard programming platform.
5. Important theory is given in brief at beginning of each topic to make clear understanding of the concepts.

Following are additions made in 2nd edition of the book.

1. Added separate chapter for discussion on File Handling concepts.
2. Added separate chapter for discussion on subjective questions asked during interview and their best possible answers.
3. The new "Miscellaneous Questions" chapters discuss dynamic memory allocations, command line arguments, bit fields, operator restriction and other miscellaneous topics from C language.

Acknowledgment

I am obliged to numerous people around for their help in planning and preparation of this book. I am thankful to Principal Dr. S. S. Kulkarni and Prof. S. S. Gramopadhey for igniting my mind to write a book that can make a difference. Many of my colleagues have been extremely supportive to me during the entire work. Prof. M. L. Deshpande in particular has been highly motivating to me while writing of the book. Many of my students with whom I had fruitful discussions, debates on various questions, answers and explanations are crucial stakeholders of the book. Finally I would like to thank all my family members for their support and constant motivation.

Table of Contents

DATA TYPES AND CONTROL STATEMENTS

Important Theory for Objective Questions:

C Language Data Types

Data types are used to store various types of data that is processed by a program. Data type attaches with variable to determine the number of bytes to be allocate to variable and valid operations which can be performed on that variable. The following are different data types supported in the C Language.

1. Fundamental/ Primitive Data Types

The primitive data types in C Language are int, float, char and void. Type modifier is used to change the meaning of primitive data types so that they can be used in different situations. The various type modifiers available in C language are- signed, unsigned, short and long. The C language offers three different 'int' type modifiers - short, int, and long which represents three different integer sizes. The C language also offers 3 different floating point type modifiers - float, double, and long double.

Two special 'char' type modifiers are- signed, unsigned.

2. Derived Data Types

Data types that are derived from fundamental data types are called derived data types. Derived data types don't create a new data type; instead, they add some functionality to the basic data types. The two very commonly used derived data types are - Array and Pointer.

3. User Defined Data Types

User defined data type is used to create new data types. The new data types formed are fundamental data types. Different user defined data types are: struct, union, enum, typedef.

We will discuss and elaborate fundamental data types in this chapter; the derived and user defined data types will be discussed in depth in the forthcoming chapters. The following are some important details of fundamental data types.

A) Character Data Type

C stores character data internally as an integer. Each character has 8 bits so we can have 256 different character values (0-255). The character data can be signed or unsigned depending on type modifier.

B) Integer Data Type

Integer data types are used to store numbers and characters. Integers have 3 types depending on memory allocated viz. short, int and long. The integer data types *short*, *long* and *int* can be either signed or unsigned depending on the range of numbers needed to be represented. Signed types can represent both positive and negative values, whereas unsigned types can only represent positive values (and zero). By default, if we do not specify either *signed* or *unsigned*, most compiler settings will assume the type to be signed.

C) Floating-point Data Type

Floating-point data types are used to represent floating-point numbers. Floating-point data types come in three sizes: float (single precision), double (double precision), and long double (extended precision). The exact meaning of single, double, and extended precision is based on the implementation defined. Floating-point literal is double by default.

You can use the suffix 'f' or 'F' to get a floating-point literal 3.14f or 3.14F.

The following table summarizes fundamental data types in C Language according to size, value range and format specifiers -:

Data Type	Format Specifer	Memory Allocation	Value Range
signed char	%c	1 Byte	-2^7 to 2^7-1 (–128 to 127)
unsigned char	%c	1 Byte	0 to 2^8-1 (0 to 255)
short	%d	2 Bytes	-2^{15} to $2^{15}-1$ (–32768 to 32767)
unsigned short	%u	2 Bytes	0 to $2^{16}-1$ (0 to 65535)
long int	%ld	4 Bytes	2^{31} to $2^{31}-1$ (2,147,483,648 to 2,147,483,647)
int	%d or %i	2 or 4 Bytes depending on platform. (we will assume 2 bytes)	Range for 2 or 4 Bytes as given above
float	%f	4 Bytes	3.4E +/- 38
double	%lf	8 Bytes	1.7E +/- 308
long double	%ld	10 Bytes	3.4 e-4932 to 3.4 e+4932

Negative Numbers:

The most significant bit (MSB) is a 1 for any negative integer (so for 8 bit numbers all negative numbers are 1XXXXXXX where X can be either 1 or 0). To invert the sign of a number, 2's complement (invert the bits and then add 1) of number is taken. So to get -127, first take 127 = 01111111, invert the bits to get 10000000 then add 1 = 10000001.

Type Conversion

Type conversion occurs when an expression has mixed data types. At this time, the compiler will try to convert from lower to higher type, because converting from higher to lower may cause loss of precision and value. The C language considers various data types in the following ways.

- Integer types are lower than floating-point types.
- Signed types are lower than unsigned types.
- Short whole-number types are lower than longer types.

The hierarchy of data types is as follows: double, float, long, int, short, char.

So based on the above, C Language has the following rules for type conversion:

- Character and short data are promoted to integer.
- Unsigned char and unsigned short are converted to unsigned integer.
- If the expression includes unsigned integer and any other data type, the other data type is converted to an unsigned integer and the result will be an unsigned integer.
- If the expression contains long and any other data type, that data type is converted to long and the result will be long.
- Float is promoted to double.
- If the expression includes long and unsigned integer data types, the unsigned integer is converted to unsigned long and the result will be unsigned long.
- If the mixed expression is of the double data type, the other operand is also converted to double and the result will be double.
- If the mixed expression is of the unsigned long data type, then the other operand is also converted to double and the result will be double.

Type Casting

When we want to convert the value of a variable from one type to another, we can use type casting. Type casting does not change the actual value of a variable.

Volatile Variable

A volatile variable is the one whose values may be changed at any time by some external sources.

Example: volatile int num;

The value of data may be altered by some external factor, even if it does not appear on the left hand side of the assignment statement. When we declare a variable as volatile the compiler will examine the value of the variable each time it is encountered to see if an external factor has changed the value.

Declaring Variable as Constant

The values of some variable may be required to remain constant through-out the program. We can do this by using the qualifier const at the time of initialization.

Example: const int a = 40;

The const data type qualifier tells the compiler that the value of the int variable 'a' cannot be modified in the program; if an attempt is made to modify the value then the compiler shows the error.

Defining Symbolic Constants

A symbolic constant value can be defined as a preprocessor statement and used in the program as any other constant value. Some examples of constant definitions are:

```
#define        max_marks        100
#define        pi               3.14159
```

These definitions may appear anywhere in the program, but must come before it is referenced in the program. It is a standard practice to place them at the beginning of the program.

Important Points-:

1. If the first digit of an integer is 0 then the integer value is considered as an Octal number.
2. E.g. If we declare an integer as -: int a = 016; then the decimal value stored in the variable 'a' is 14. ($6x8^0+1x8^1=14$).
3. To store hexadecimal values in an integer; use the prefix 0x to the value.
4. E.g. If we declare integer as -: int a = 0x16; then the decimal value stored in the variable 'a' is 22. ($6x16^0+1x16^1=22$).
5. The C compilers use 'double' as default data type for all floating point constants.
6. The execution of 'for' loop goes in the order -: Initialization, check the condition, loop body and then looping expression.
7. In 'switch' statement, the argument can be either an integer, character or an expression that evaluates to an integer. The 'case' keyword follows either an integer constant, character constant or a constant expression that evaluates to an integer.

† Objective Questions

Que. 1.1) Predicate the output. | **Rough work space.**

```
#include<stdio.h>
void main()
{
    unsigned i=-1;
    printf("%d ",i);
    printf("\t%u ",i);
}
```

A.	1 0
B.	Garbage Values
C.	-1 65535
D.	1 -1

Que. 1.2) Predicate the output. | **Rough work space.**

```
#include<stdio.h>
void main()
{
    unsigned i=-1;
    int j;
    printf("%u ",++i);
    j=--i;
    printf("%u   %d",j,j);
}
```

A.	0 1 Garbage
B.	65535 0 -1
C.	-1 65535 0
D.	0 65535 -1

Que.1.3) Predicate the output.	Rough work space.

#include<stdio.h>
void main()
{
int a=32767;
printf("%d",a);
a++;
printf(" %d",a);
a++;
printf(" %d",a);
a++;
printf(" %d",a);
}	

A.	32767 -32768 -32767 -32766
B.	Garbage Value
C.	-32768 -32767 -32766 32768
D.	32767 32768 32769 32770

Que.1.4) Predicate the output.	Rough work space.

#include<stdio.h>
void main()
{
unsigned int i=10;
while(i-->=0)
printf("%u ",i);
}	

A.	10 9 8 7 6 5 4 3 2 1 0
B.	Infinite loop printing garbage values.
C.	10 9 8 7 6 5 4 3 2 1 0 65535 65534 .....
D.	10 9 8 7 6 5 4 3 2 1

Que.1.5) Predicate the output.	Rough work space.

#include<stdio.h>
void main()
{
unsigned int i;
for(i=1;i>-2;i--)
printf("Hello");
}	

A.	Hello
B.	Infinite display of "Hello"
C.	Hello Hello
D.	Do not display anything.

Que.1.6) Predicate the output.	Rough work space.

#include<stdio.h>
void main()
{
unsigned int i=65000;
while(i++!=0);
printf("%d",i);
}	

A.	1
B.	0
C.	65000
D.	65001

Que.1.7) Predicate the output.	Rough work space.

#include<stdio.h>
void main()
{
    int i=0,j=200;
    while(i<j)
    {
        --j;
        i+=2;
    }
    printf("%d", i-j);
}	

A.	0
B.	1
C.	-1
D.	2

Que.1.8) Predicate the output.	Rough work space.

#include<stdio.h>
void main()
{
    int a=1;
    switch(a)
    {
        int k=1;
        case 1: printf("%d",k);
                break;
        default: printf("%d",k);
                break;
    }
}	

A.	1
B.	0
C.	Garbage Value
D.	2

Que.1.9) Predicate the output.	**Rough work space.**

#include<stdio.h>
void main()
{
int cnt=5,a=1000;
do
{
a/=cnt;
}while(cnt--);
printf("%d",a);
}	

A.	1
B.	0
C.	2
D.	Divide by zero error.

Que.1.10) What should be condition to print the message "HelloWorld"?	**Rough work space.**

if "condition"
printf("Hello");
else
printf("World");	

A.	!printf("Hello")
B.	printf("Hello")
C.	printf("HelloWorld")
D.	None of above.

Que.1.11) What input should be given in following program to print "yes"?	**Rough work space.**

```
#include<stdio.h>
void main()
{
        int i,j;
        scanf("%d%d",&i,&j);
        i+=2;
        j-=2;
        if( (i=5) && ( j=-3))
                printf("yes");
        else
                printf("no");
}
```

A.	i=10 and j=20
B.	i=100 and j=200
C.	Any input.
D.	i=1 and j=2

Que.1.12) Predicate the output.	**Rough work space.**

```
#include<stdio.h>
void main()
{
        int x=10,y=20,z;
        if(y<0)  if(y>0)  x=30;
        else      x=50;
        printf("%d",x);
}
```

A.	30
B.	10
C.	50
D.	Garbage Value

Que. 1.13) Predicate the output.	Rough work space.

#include<stdio.h>
void main()
{
for(;;)
printf("Hello");
}	

A.	"Hello"
B.	Nothing
C.	Infinite loop printing "Hello"
D.	Compiler Error

Que. 1.14) Predicate the output.	Rough work space.

#include<stdio.h>
void main()
{
while()
printf("Hello");
}	

A.	"Hello"
B.	Nothing
C.	Infinite loop printing "Hello"
D.	Compiler Error

Que. 1.15) Predicate the output.	Rough work space.

#include<stdio.h>
void main()
{
float a=0.9;
if(a==0.9)
printf("Hello");
else
printf("Hi");
}	

A.	Hi
B.	Hello

C.	Compiler Error
D.	None of above.

Que. 1.16) Predicate the output.	Rough work space.

#include<stdio.h>
void main()
{
printf("%d %d %d",sizeof(0.9f),
sizeof(0.9),sizeof(0.9l));
}	

A.	4 4 4
B.	4 8 10
C.	4 6 8
D.	2 4 6

Que. 1.17) Predicate the output.	Rough work space.

#include<stdio.h>
void main()
{
float a=0.9;
switch(a)
{
case 1.2: printf("Hello");
case 0.7: printf("Hi");
}
}	

A.	Hello
B.	Compiler Error
C.	Hi
D.	HelloHi

Que. 1.18) Predicate the output.	Rough work space.

#include<stdio.h>
void main()
{
    float f = 1.1;
    double d = 1.1;
    if(f==d)
printf("Hello");
   else
        printf("Hi");
}	

A.	Hi
B.	Compiler Error
C.	Hello
D.	HelloHi

Que. 1.19) Predicate the output.	Rough work space.

#include<stdio.h>
void main()
{
        int a=7;
switch(a)
{
default:printf("All");
case 7: printf("Hello");
case 10:printf("Hi");
}
}	

A.	Hello
B.	Compiler Error
C.	AllHelloHi
D.	HelloHi

Que. 1.20) Predicate when the output of the following Code will be "Hello".	Rough work space.

```
#include<stdio.h>
void main()
{
        int a=10,b,c;
if( a && scanf("%d%d",&b,&c))
printf("Hello");
        else
printf("Hi");
}
```

A.	If a=1 and b=2
B.	Always
C.	Never
D.	If a=0 and b=0

Que. 1.21) Predicate the output.	Rough work space.

```
#include<stdio.h>
void main()
{
        int i=10;
        while (i<=50)
        {
                printf("%d",i);
                if (i>2)
                        goto there;
                i++;
        }
}
fun()
{
        there:
                printf("Hello");
}
```

A.	Compiler Error
B.	1Hello
C.	1
D.	Hello

Que. 1.22) Predicate the output.	**Rough work space.**

#include<stdio.h>
void main()
{
    int i=1,j=2;
    switch(i)
    {
    case 1: printf("Hello");
        break;
    case j: printf("Hi");
        break;
    }
}	

A.	Hello
B.	Hi
C.	Compiler Error
D.	Nothing

Que. 1.23) Predicate the output.	**Rough work space.**

void main()
{
    int i;
    printf("%d",scanf("%d",&i));//Input
//i=1000
}	

A.	3
B.	2
C.	1
D.	Garbage

Que. 1.24) Predicate the output.	**Rough work space.**

#include<stdio.h>
void main()
{
while(1)
{
if(printf("%d",printf("%d")))
break;
else
continue;
}
}	

A.	Garbage Value
B.	Garbage Values infinitely
C.	Nothing
D.	1 1

Que. 1.25) Predicate the output.	**Rough work space.**

#include<stdio.h>
void main()
{
int x,y=2,z,a;
if(x=y%2) z=2;
a=2;
printf("%d %d ",z,x);
}	

A.	2 0
B.	Garbage 0
C.	2 Garbage
D.	2 2

Que. 1.26) Predicate the output.	Rough work space.

#include<stdio.h>
void main()
{
    for(;0;)
        printf("Hello ");
}	

A.	Garbage
B.	Compiler Error
C.	Nothing
D.	Hello

Que. 1.27) Predicate the output.	Rough work space.

#include<stdio.h>
void main()
{
    for(;1;)
        printf("Hello ");
}	

A.	Garbage
B.	Compiler Error
C.	Nothing
D.	Hello printed infinitely

† Answers with Explanation

Answer 1.1	C. -1 65535
Explanation 1.1	The '%d' format specifier is useful for signed integer variable; hence first printf() displays the correct value of variable 'i'. The '%u' format specifier considers the value in unsigned integer form. The value -1 is a negative number, hence 2's complement of the number 1 is stored in the memory (which is 1111 1111 1111 1111). Due to %u format specifier the sign bit (i.e. MSB) is neglected in the binary value and number is treated as a positive number. The binary representation 1111 1111 1111 1111 is equivalent to 65535.

Answer 1.2	D. 0 65535 -1
Explanation 1.2	Note the different format specifiers used in the printf() statement and apply the same explanation given in 1.1.

Answer 1.3	A. 32767 -32768 -32767 -32766
Explanation 1.3	We assume that 'int' takes 2 bytes for storage. The variable 'a' is a signed integer; hence it takes 1 bit to store sign and 15 bits to store magnitude (actual value). The 32767 is the largest positive value that can be stored in an integer which has binary presentation as 0111 1111 1111 1111. Adding 1 to this binary presentation results into 1000 0000 0000 0000 which is -32768 (i.e. 2's complement of 32768).

Answer 1.4	**C.10 9 8 7 6 5 4 3 2 1 0 65535 65534.....**
Explanation 1.4	In the code 'i' is an unsigned integer, so it never becomes negative number. So the condition in 'while' is always true, this leads to an infinite loop. Note -: As variable 'i' is 'unsigned int' so we have used the '%u' format specifier. The output is different if we use the '%d' format specifer which is applicable for signed integers.

Answer 1.5	**D. This code does not display anything.**
Explanation 1.5	In the code 'i' is an unsigned integer. The variable 'i' is compared with a signed value. Since the both data types don't match, the signed value is automatically promoted to an unsigned value. The unsigned equivalent of -2 is a huge value, so the condition becomes false and the control comes out of the loop.

Answer 1.6	**A.1**
Explanation 1.6	In the code note the semicolon after the 'while' statement. When the value of 'i' becomes 0, it comes out of the while loop. Due to post-increment on 'i', the value of 'i' becomes 1 after exiting the loop.

Answer 1.7	**B.1**
Explanation 1.7	Trace the execution of the 'for' loop with values of 'i' and 'j'. The difference between values is 1 when the 'for' loop terminates.

Answer 1.8	**C. Garbage value**
Explanation 1.8	In the switch statement the value of variable 'a' is 1; hence all instructions till control reaches to "case 1" are simply ignored. Hence variable 'k' remains un-initialized.

Answer 1.9	D.Error : Run time error (Divide by zero).
Explanation 1.9	In the code, the post-decrement operator used in 'do-while' condition. The value of 'cnt' becomes 0 in the last iteration of the loop. Hence it results into "Divide By Zero" error.

Answer 1.10	A.!printf("Hello");
Explanation 1.10	In the code, printf("Hello") displays the string "Hello" and returns value 5 (number of characters printed). Due to '!' operator, non-zero value returned by printf() i.e. 5 gets converted into 0. Hence else condition of 'if' is executed.

Answer 1.11	C.Any input. It always prints "yes".
Explanation 1.11	Please note that in 'if' condition, we have used the assignment (=) operator and not the comparison operator (==). Here both variables are initialized with non-zero values; hence 'if' condition becomes always TRUE.

Answer 1.12	B.10

Explanation 1.12	The above code is equivalent to -:
	if(y<0)
	{
	if(y>0)
	x=30;
	else
	x=50;
	}

Answer 1.13	C.Infinite loop printing "Hello".
Explanation 1.13	The initiation, condition and post-increment / post-decrement is optional in the 'for' loop. In the 'for' loop none of the above three value is given; hence the loop executes infinitely.

Answer 1.14	**D.Compilation Error.**
Explanation 1.14	The condition in the 'while' statement is essential; this is different from the 'for' loop where it is optional.

Answer 1.15	**A.Hi**
Explanation 1.15	In the code, variable 'a' is a float variable. The value 0.9 is by default considered with double precession. Hence the data stored internally is not the same for both variables.

Answer 1.16	**B. 4 8 10**
Explanation 1.16	The '0.9f' is considered as float value, '0.9' is considered as double value and '0.9l' is considered as long double. Hence the printf() displays memory reserved for float, double and long double data types.

Answer 1.17	**B. Compilation Error**
Explanation 1.17	In the "switch" block, we can use either integer or character values for a "case" statement. The float value is not permitted in "case".

Answer 1.18	**A. Hi**
Explanation 1.18	The value stored in memory cannot be predicted exactly for a floating point data (E.g. float, double, long double). The precision of the the stored value depends on the number of bytes reserved for the storage. The float variable occupies 4 bytes and long double occupies 10 bytes. So the float stores the given number with less precision than a long double. Note: Never compare or at-least be cautious when using floating point numbers with relational operators (== , >, <, <=, >=,!=)

Answer 1.19	**D. HelloHi**
Explanation 1.19	In the code, the "default" case is given as first statement in the "switch" block. The "default" executes only when no other "case" satisfies. Also note that, the 'break' is not used after each "case" statement.

Answer 1.20	**B. Always Hello**
Explanation 1.20	The scanf() function returns the number of values scanned/read successfully. In the code, scanf() returns value 2 which is a non-zero value; hence condition of the 'if' is always TRUE.

Answer 1.21	**A. Compiler error: Undefined label 'there' in function main.**
Explanation 1.21	The "label" have function's scope, in other words the scope of the "label" is limited to a function. The label "there" is available in function "fun"; Hence it is not visible in the "main" function.

Answer 1.22	**C. Compiler Error: Constant expression required in function main.**
Explanation 1.22	The "case" statement in the "switch" block can use constant expressions only. This implies that, we cannot use variable names directly in the "case" statement. So an error is raised by the compiler. Note: Enumerated types can be used in case statements

Answer 1.23	**C. 1**
Explanation 1.23	The scanf() returns the number of items read successfully. Here the value 1000 is given as input which is scanned successfully. So the number of items read is 1.

Answer 1.24	A. Garbage values
Explanation 1.24	The inner printf() executes initially to print some garbage value. The inner printf() returns the number of characters printed and this value cannot be predicted in the given code. The value returned by inner printf() acts as argument to the outer printf(); hence the outer printf() prints something and returns a non-zero value. Due to this, it encounters the "break" statement and comes out of the "while" block.

Answer 1.25	B. Garbage-value 0
Explanation 1.25	The value of y%2 is 0. This value is assigned to the variable 'x'. The condition reduces to "if(x)" or in other words "if(0)" and so the variable 'z' remains uninitialized.

Answer 1.26	D. "Hello" is printed once.
Explanation 1.26	In the code, the value '0' is present as a condition of the 'for' loop. Hence the loop terminates after the first iteration.

Answer 1.27	D. "Hello" is printed infinitely.
Explanation 1.27	The value '1' is present as the condition of the 'for' loop; hence the loop never terminates.

Chapter

2

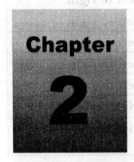

OPERATORS AND EXPRESSIONS

Important Theory for Objective Questions:

The C language supports the following type of operators-:

- Arithmetic Operators (+,-,*,/,%,++,--)
- Logical (or Relational) Operators (==,!=,<,>,>=,<=,&&,| |,!)
- Bitwise Operators (&,!,^,>>,<<,~)
- Assignment Operators (=,+=,-=,*=,/=,%=,<<=,>>=,&=,^=,!=)
- Misc Operators (sizeof(), ?: ,&, *)

The operator precedence and associativity is as given in the following table. The *associtivity* indicates order in which operators of equal precedence are applied. The following table gives the information about various operators available in C with their priorities and associtivity.

OPERATORS	ASSOCIATIVITY
( ) [ ] -> .	left to right
! ~ ++ -- + - * & (type) sizeof	right to left
* / %	left to right
+ -	left to right
<< >>	left to right
< <= > >=	left to right
== ! =	left to right
&	left to right
^	left to right
¦	left to right
&&	left to right
¦ ¦	left to right
? :	right to left
= += - = *= /= %= &= ^= ¦ = <<= >>=	right to left
,	left to right

Table 2.1: Precedence And Associativity Of Operators

In the above table operators from same row have same precedence e.g. the operators '/', '*' and '%' all have same priority. The rows are in order of decreasing precedence e.g. '++' operator have more precedence than operator '<<'.

The associtivity indicates order in which operators of equal precedence are applied. The operators '*', '/' and '%' are having same priority and left to right associtivity.

E.g. Consider the expression x= 20*10/5;

In above expression after applying associtivity rule the order of operator evaluation is '*' and then '/' (due to left to right associtivity). Hence the above expression is evaluated as -: x= (20*10)/5 = 40.

E.g. Consider the expression x= 20/10*5;

In above expression after applying associtivity rule the order of operator evaluation is '/' and then '*' (due to left to right associtivity). Hence the above expression is evaluated as -: x= (20/10)*5 = 10.

Rules for evaluation of C Language expression-:

- First parenthesized sub expressions are evaluated from left to right.
- If parentheses are nested, the evaluation begins with the innermost sub expression.
- The precedence rule is applied in determining the order of application of operators in evaluating sub expressions.
- The associability rule is applied when two or more operators of the same precedence level appear in the sub expression.

Important Points:

For Logical And (&&) operator, the second condition is evaluated only if the first condition is TRUE. This is done because of (0 && ANYTHING) is always FALSE.

For Logical Or (||) operator, the second condition is not evaluated if the first condition is TRUE. This is done because of (1 || ANYTHING) is always TRUE.

In the expression y=++x, the value of 'x' is updated first and then stored in 'y'. Similar things are applicable to pre-decrement (--).

In the expression y=x++, ++ (post-increment) is converted into two expressions as y=x; and then x++. This will be explained in details below in 2.13.

The comma operator (',') is evaluated from left to right. All side effects of evaluations of the left operand is completed before evaluation of the right operand. The value of the right most sub-expression is taken as the final result of expression. The concept of sequence point is explained in detail in 2.13.

The expression x+=1 is equivalent to x=x+1.

The value 0 is considered to be the Boolean value 'FALSE', and any non-zero value is considered to be the Boolean value 'TRUE'. This is very important in evaluation of 'if' and applying Logical operators.

E.g. 1)
```
x=-10;
if(x)
printf("Hello");
```
In the above code, if condition evaluates to TRUE as value of x is Non-Zero.

2)
```
x=!10;
```

The '!' is a logical operator and 10 is a non-zero value. So !10 is equivalent to 'FALSE'. Hence value '0' is stored in the variable 'x'.

The value of "const" variable can't be changed; if such an attempt is made in the code, the compiler shows an error.

In C language the *modulus(%)* operator can be applied only on integers and characters (as characters are stored as numbers internally) and not on the float or double values. If anyone tries to use the modulus operator on floats or double then the compiler would display the error message as *'Illegal use of Floating Point'*.

The conditional expression given as: *expression1 ? expression2 : expression3.*

Here *expression1* is evaluated first. If it returns non-zero value then, only *expression2* is evaluated; otherwise only *expression3* is evaluated.

The "sizeof" is an operator.

The C language standard does not specify the order in which operands of an operator are evaluated. The exception for this are &&, | | , ?: and , operators.

E.g. ans= f1() + f2();

In the above expression whether function f1() is evaluated (called) first or function f2() is not fixed. The order of evaluation in such a case may be different for different compilers.

Side Effects and Sequence point

If an expression, in addition to assigning a value to the variable also modifies some other variable's content, then expression is said to have a side affect.

E.g. y=x++;

The above expression assigns the new value to variable 'y'. The above expression also modifies the value of 'x' which is a side effect.

A sequence point defines any point in a program's execution at which it is guaranteed that all side effects of previous evaluations have been performed, and no side effects from subsequent evaluations have yet been performed.

E.g. Consider expression y=x++; wherein ++ is post-increment.

Here variable 'y' stores the old value of 'x'. The side effect of changing the value of 'x' (post-increment) is evaluated only after ';' sequence point. Hence the value of 'x' changes after reaching to ';' sequence point.

The following are valid sequence points in C program-:

Between evaluation of the left and right operands of the &&, || and comma operators.
E.g. if (condition1 && condition2)
In the above statement, the condition2 is evaluated after applying side effects of condition1 (and if condition1 is TRUE).

Between the evaluation of the first operand of the Conditional operator and the second or third operand.

At the end of a full expression. E.g. The assignment a=b; or return statements, the controlling expressions of if, switch, while, or do-while statements, and all three expressions in a for statement.

Before a function is entered in a function call.

At a function return, after the return value is copied into the calling context.

14. Consider expression a[i]=i++;

It is important to find that, whether array subscript in the above expression takes old or new value of variable 'i'? Answer to this question is compiler dependent. This is intentionally kept aside in the standards since the best order of evaluation always depends on machine architecture.

† Objective Questions

Que. 2.1) Predicate the output. | **Rough work space.**

```
#include<stdio.h>
void main()
{
        int i=0,j=2,k=0;
        if( i && (j=i++))
                k=1;
        printf("%d %d %d",i,j,k);
}
```

A.	0 1 1
B.	0 2 0
C.	0 0 1
D.	1 0 1

Que. 2.2) Predicate the output. | **Rough work space.**

```
#include<stdio.h>
void main()
{
        int i=-5,j=1,k=-3,r;
        r=i++ && (--j || k++);
        printf("%d %d %d
%d",i,j,k,r);
}
```

A.	-4 0 -2 1
B.	-4 0 1 1
C.	-4 0 -2 0
D.	None of above.

Que.2.3) What you would write in the blank to output "YES"?	Rough work space.

#include<stdio.h>
void main()
{
    int i=1;
    if(i--,_______)
        printf("YES");
    else
        printf("No");
}	

A.	0
B.	i
C.	--i
D.	++i

Que.2.4) Predicate the output.	Rough work space.

#include<stdio.h>
void main()
{
    int i=-1,j=-2,k;
    k=-i++ * ++j;
    printf("%d %d %d",i,j,k);
}	

A.	0 -1 -1
B.	0 0 -1
C.	1 0 1
D.	1 1 1

Que.2.5) Predicate the output.	Rough work space.

#include<stdio.h>
void main()
{
int i=-1,k=3;
k=(i++ && i++) ? ++i :i++;
printf("%d %d",i,k);
}	

A.	1 2
B.	1 1
C.	2 1
D.	2 2

Que.2.6) Predicate the output.	Rough work space.

#include<stdio.h>
void main()
{
int i=0;
int r=++i++;
printf("%d",r);
}	

A.	2
B.	1
C.	0
D.	Compiler Error

Que.2.7) Predicate the output.
#include<stdio.h>
void main()
{
int i=-1,j=-2,k=0,l=1,m;
m = i++ && j++ && k++ ||
l++;
printf("%d %d %d %d
%d",i,j,k,l,m);
}
	Rough work space.

A.	0 1 2 2 1
B.	1 -1 1 2 1
C.	0 -1 1 2 1
D.	0 -1 1 2 0

Que.2.8) Predicate the output.
#include<stdio.h>
void main()
{
int i=0;
for(;i<20 && printf("%d ",i); i++);
{
switch(i)
{ case 0: i++;i*=2;
case 20: i+=2;
case 70: i+=6;
default: i+=3;
}
}
}
	Rough work space.

A.	0 14 18
B.	1 15 19
C.	0 13 17
D.	0 14 19

Que.2.9) Predicate the output.	**Rough work space.**

#include<stdio.h>
void main()
{
    int i=2,j=3,k;
    k=i+++j;
    printf("%d %d %d",i,j,k);
}	

A.	3 3 5
B.	3 3 3
C.	2 3 5
D.	3 3 4

Que.2.10) Write down code to set 5th and 7th bit of binary representation of integer 'n'.

Que.2.11) Predicate the output.	**Rough work space.**

#include<stdio.h>
void main()
{
    int i=2,j,k;
    i *= 3+2;
    printf("%d",i);
    i *= j = k=4;
    print("%d",i);
}	

A.	8 4
B.	8 16
C.	10 40
D.	10 16

Que.2.12) Predicate the output.	**Rough work space.**

#include<stdio.h>
void main()
{
int i=3,j=2,k=1;
print("%d", i | j & k);
print("%d",i | j & ~k);
i=1;
i<<=3;
print("%d",i);
}	

A.	2 3 8
B.	3 3 3
C.	3 3 8
D.	3 2 8

Que. 2.13) Predicate the output.	**Rough work space.**

#include<stdio.h>
void main()
{
printf("%x",-1<<4);
}	

A.	0xFF00
B.	0xFFFF
C.	0x0000
D.	0xFFF0

Que. 2.14) Predicate the output.	**Rough work space.**

#include<stdio.h>
void main()
{
int i= - - 2;
printf("i=%d",i);
}	

A.	i=0
B.	i=-2
C.	Compiler Error
D.	i=2

Que. 2.15) Predicate the output.
#include<stdio.h>
void main()
{
int i=10;
i=!i>14;
printf ("i=%d",i);
}
	Rough work space.

A.	i=1
B.	i=0
C.	i=10
D.	i=14

Que. 2.16) Predicate the output.
#include<stdio.h>
void main()
{
int i;
i=(100>200)==1;
printf("%d",i);
i=!10>3;
printf("%d",i);
}
	Rough work space.

A.	1 1
B.	0 0
C.	0 1
D.	1 0

Que. 2.17) Predicate the output.
#include<stdio.h>
void main()
{
int i=5;
t = i+++++i;
printf("%d",t);
}
	Rough work space.

A.	Compiler Error
B.	11
C.	10
D.	12

Que. 2.18) Predicate the output.	**Rough work space.**

#include<stdio.h>
void main()
{
int i=-1;
+i;
printf("%d %d ",i,+i);
}	

A.	-1 1
B.	1 1
C.	-1 -1
D.	1 Garbage

Que. 2.19) Predicate the output.	**Rough work space.**

#include<stdio.h>
void main()
{
char not;
not=!2;
printf("%d",not);
}	

A.	0
B.	1
C.	2
D.	Garbage Value

Que. 2.20) Predicate the output.	**Rough work space.**

#include<stdio.h>
void main()
{
int k=1;
printf("%d==1 is
""%s",k,k==1?"TRUE":"FALSE");
}	

A.	1==1 is FALSE
B.	1==0 is TRUE
C.	1==1 is TRUE
D.	0==1 is TRUE

Que. 2.21) Predicate the output.	Rough work space.

#include<stdio.h>
void main()
{
int j;
scanf("%d",&j); // input given is 2000
if((j%4==0 && j%100 != 0) || j%100 == 0)
printf("%d is a leap year",j);
else
printf("%d is not a leap year",j);
}	

A.	Compiler Error
B.	2000 is not a leap year.
C.	2000 is a leap year.
D.	None of above.

Que. 2.22) Predicate the output.	Rough work space.

#include<stdio.h>
void main()
{
int i=-1;
-i;
printf("%d %d",i,-i);
}	

A.	1 1
B.	-1 1
C.	-1 -1
D.	1 -1

Que. 2.23) Predicate the output.	Rough work space.

#include<stdio.h>
void main()
{
const int i=4;
float j;
j = ++i;
printf("%d %f", i,++j);
}	

A.	4 5.0
B.	5 6.0

C.	Run Time Error
D.	Compiler Error

Que. 2.24) Predicate the output.	**Rough work space.**

```
#include<stdio.h>
void main()
{
int i=5,j=6,k;
printf("%d",i+++j);
}
```

A.	10
B.	11
C.	12
D.	Compiler Error

Que. 2.25) Predicate the output.	**Rough work space.**

```
#include<stdio.h>
void main()
{
 int i =0;j=0;
 if(i && j++)
      printf("%d  %d",i++,j);
printf("  %d  %d",i,j);
}
```

A.	0 0
B.	0 0 1 1
C.	0 0 0 1
D.	0 0 0 0

Que. 2.26) Predicate the output.	**Rough work space.**

#include<stdio.h>
void main()
{
int k=ret(sizeof(float));
printf("%d",++k);
}
int ret(int ret)
{
ret += 2.5;
return(ret);
}	

A.	3
B.	6
C.	7
D.	Compiler Error

Que. 2.27) Predicate the output.	**Rough work space.**

#include<stdio.h>
void main()
{
int a= 0;
int b = 20;
char x =1;
char y =10;
if(a,b,x,y)
printf("hello");
else
printf("hi");
}	

A.	Compiler Error
B.	Hi
C.	Nothing
D.	hello

† Answers to Objective Questions0

Answer 2.1	B. 0 2 0
Explanation 2.1	In the code value of the variable 'i' is 0, hence the second condition in '&&' is not evaluated. Due to this, the expression inside parenthesis results to 0. Hence 'if' condition is not satisfied; so all values remains as it is.

Answer 2.2	A. -4 0 -2 1
Explanation 2.2	In the code evaluation is carried out as: r= -5 && (0 || -3) r= -5 && 1 (Since -3 is a non-zero value, the result of 0 || -3 = 1) r=1 (as both arguments for && are non-zero values). After evaluation of the 'r', post-increment of the 'i' and 'k' is carried out.

Answer 2.3	D.++i OR !i
Explanation 2.3	The value of variable 'i' becomes zero when the comma operator in 'if' is reached. To make the value of 'i' equal to one (so that the 'if' condition will become TRUE) either of the above expressions can be used. Please note that, the result of the second operand of comma operator is taken into consideration for the 'if' condition.

Answer 2.4	A. 0 -1 -1
Explanation 2.4	The expression is evaluated as follows-: k= 1 * -1 as the unary minus ('-') has more precedence than post-increment (++). And after evalution of the variable 'k', the value of variable 'i' is incremented by 1.

Answer 2.5	**C. 2 1**
Explanation 2.5	The expression is evaluated as follows-: k= (-1 && 0) ? ++i : i++;(please note that '&&' is valid sequence points. Hence the value of 'i' is updated immediately. The result of the conditional operator is false.) k= i++; (Since '?' is a valid sequence point, after evaluation of the condition 'i' becomes 1). Hence k=1 and i=2

Answer 2.6	**D. Compiler Error : LVALUE required**
Explanation 2.6	In the expression r=++i++ for the postfix '++' operator, the left side is not an addressable expression.

Answer 2.7	**C. 0 -1 1 2 1**
Explanation 2.7	The expression is evaluated as follows-: m= -1 && -2 && 0 || 1; (++ and -- has more precedence than && and ||) m= 1 && 0 || 1; (&& has more precedence than || and it's associtivity is from left to right.) m= 0 || 1; Hence m=1; value of variables i,j,k,l is incremented after reaching to ';'.

Answer 2.8	**A. 0 14 18**
Explanation 2.8	The printf() function returns the number of characters sent to the output screen. In the first iteration of 'for' loop the variable i=0, hence printf() prints value '1' and returns value 1. In the "switch" block "break" statement is not used, hence all conditions are evaluated and the value of variable 'i' becomes13. When the loop goes for a second iteration 'i' becomes 14 due to i++. Here printf() prints the value '14' and returns the value 2(as 2 characters printed). The 'for' loop continue execution in the similar way.

<table>
<tr><td>Answer 2.9</td><td>A. 3 3 5</td></tr>
<tr><td>Explanation 2.9</td><td>The expression is evaluated as follows-:
k= i++ + j;
k= 2 + 3. And the variable 'i' stores value 3.</td></tr>
</table>

<table>
<tr><td>Answer 2.10</td><td>n = n | (1<<4)
n= n | (1<<6)</td></tr>
<tr><td>Explanation 2.10</td><td>The expression: n = n | (1<<4) sets 5th bit of 'n' to 1.

In the above expression, bitwise shift operation is used to get a number whose 5th bit is set. Then this number is bitwise OR'ed with 'n'.

The expression: n = n | (1<<6) sets 7th bit of 'n' to 1.</td></tr>
</table>

<table>
<tr><td>Answer 2.11</td><td>C. 10 40</td></tr>
<tr><td>Explanation 2.11</td><td>The '+' operator has more precedence than *=. (Please see Operator Precedence Table 2.1)

The expression is evaluated as -:

i *= 3+2;

i *= 5;

i =10;

i *=4;(Here '=' and '*=' both have the same precedence, but due to associtivity rule evaluation is carried from right to left.)

i=40;</td></tr>
</table>

<table>
<tr><td>Answer 2.12</td><td>C. 3 3 8</td></tr>
<tr><td>Explanation 2.12</td><td>The bitwise and (&) has more precedence than the bitwise or(|). Also bitwise not(~) operator has more precedence than bitwise and(&). Hence first expression is evaluated as-:
i | (j & k)

The second expression is evaluated as -:
i | (j & (~k))</td></tr>
</table>

Answer 2.13	**D. 0xFFF0**
Explanation 2.13	The negative numbers are stored in the 2's complement form in memory. Hence the number -1 is internally represented as all 1's in binary form (As 1 in decimal is equivalent to 0000 0000 0000 0001 in binary and 2's complement of it is 1111 1111 1111 1111). If we left shift above binary value four times, the least significant 4 bits are filled with four 0's. The %x format is used to print the value of the number in hexadecimal format.

Answer 2.14	**D. i=2**
Explanation 2.14	In the expression "- -2", the unary minus (or negation) operator is used twice. Hence it results into a positive value of the variable. Note that, we cannot write the above expression as "--2". Because '--' is post-decrement operator which can not be applied on constants. The value '2' is a constant number and not a variable. Hence if we write "--2", the compiler shows an error.

Answer 2.15	**B. i=0**
Explanation 2.15	The '!' is unary logical operator. In the expression '!i>14' , the '!' operator has more precedence than '>' operator. The expression '!i' (!10) is 0 (not of true is false) and 0>14 is false (zero).

Answer 2.16	**B. 0 0**
Explanation 2.16	The expression "100>200" result to value 0. The expression 0==1 result into 0. In same way, the expression '!10>3' results to 0.

Answer 2.17	**A. Compiler Error.**
Explanation 2.17	The expression i+++++i is parsed as i++ ++ + i which is an illegal combination of operators. If the expression is modified as following (while typing) then the compiler does not show any error. t=i++ + ++i; (Please note space after the first ++ and then after the third +) In the above expression the binary operator '+' has two operands 'i++' and '++i' . As discussed in the *Important Point 2.12* the order of evaluation of operands of the operators is not fixed and is compiler dependent. The Turbo C compiler evaluates the second operand first and then the first operand. Hence the value stored in the variable 't' is 12.

Answer 2.18	**D. -1 -1**
Explanation 2.18	The unary '+' is a dummy operator in C. Whereever it comes, you can ignore it as it has no effect in the expressions.

Answer 2.19	**A. 0**
Explanation 2.19	Please read the Important Point 2.7.

Answer 2.20	**C. 1==1 is TRUE**
Explanation 2.20	When two strings are placed one after another (or separated by white-space), then they are concatenated. So the resultant string is -: "%d==1 is %s". In the code, the conditional operator (?:) evaluates to "TRUE".

Answer 2.21	**C. 2000 is a leap year**
Explanation 2.21	This is a program to check if given year is a leap year or not.

Answer 2.22	**B. -1 1**
Explanation 2.22	In the code, the second instruction '-i' doesn't affect the value of 'i'. In the printf(), the value of 'i' printed first. After that the value of the expression -i = -(-1)=1 is printed.

Answer 2.23	**D. Compiler error**
Explanation 2.23	The variable 'i' is a constant variable. The value of 'i' can't be changed.

Answer 2.24	**B. 11**
Explanation 2.24	The expression i+++j is evaluated as i++ + j.

Answer 2.25	**A.0 0**
Explanation 2.25	The value of the variable 'i' is 0. This information is enough to determine the truth value of the Boolean expression. Hence the statement following the 'if' statement is not executed. The values of 'i' and 'j' remain unchanged and get printed.

Answer 2.26	**C. 7**
Explanation 2.26	In the code, the "int ret(int ret)" is used. The function name and the argument name can be same. The function ret() is called initially to which the value 4 (sizeof(float)) is passed as argument. The ret() function returns value 6 which is pre incremented to print the value 7.

Answer 2.27	**D. hello**
Explanation 2.27	The 'comma' operator has associativity from left to right. The rightmost value is considered for evaluation of 'if' condition. Thus the value of the last variable in 'if' condition i.e. 'y' is used to evaluate the 'if'. Since the value is a non-zero value, the 'if' condition becomes true.

STORAGE CLASSES AND FUNCTIONS

Important Theory for Objective Questions:

We will start the discussion after stating the difference between *definition* and *declaration* of a variable or function. The declaration talks about the properties of a variable (primarily data type) or prototype of a function. The Definition means where a variable or function is defined in reality and actual memory is allocated for a variable or function.

A storage class defines the scope and life time of variables within a C Program. An identifier's scope determines the portions of the program in which it can be referenced. The lifetime is the period during execution of a program in which a variable or function exists in the memory.

There are 4 storage classes which can be used in a C Program-:

1) Auto - Storage Class

The **'auto'** is the default storage class for all local variables. This storage class can only be used within functions, i.e. local variables. The auto variables are automatically initialized to garbage value if not initialized explicitly. The scope of an auto variable is limited to function or a block in which the variable is declared. The lifetime of an auto variable is limited to function in which the variable is declared.

2) Register - Storage Class

The **'register'** is used to define local variables that should be stored in a register instead of RAM. This means that the variable has a maximum size equal to the register size (usually one word) and can't have the unary '&' operator applied to it (as it does not have a memory location).

E.g. register int count;

The register storage class should only be used for variables that require quick access - such as counters. It should also be noted that defining 'register' does not mean that the variable will be stored in a register. It means that it may be stored in a register - depending on hardware and implementation restrictions. The register variables are automatically initialized to garbage value if not initialized explicitly. The scope and lifetime of a register variable is the same as that of an auto variable.

3) Static storage class

The variable from a function can be declared as a 'static' variable. If this is done the variable is initialized at run time but is not reinitialized when the function is called. This static variable retains its value during various function calls. The static variables are initialized to 0 automatically. The scope of static variable is limited to a function in which the variable is declared. The lifetime of a static variable is equivalent to the lifetime of the program.

4)Extern storage Class

The **extern** storage class is used to give a reference of a global variable that is visible to all program files. When we use 'extern' keyword with the variable then that variable cannot be initialized as all it does is point the variable name at a storage location that has been previously defined.

When we have multiple files with a few global variables or functions which will be used in different files, then *extern* is useful in another file to give reference of a defined variable or function.

Important Points:

The program execution always starts from the main() function. In other words, main() is the entry point of C Program.

By default return type of function in C Language is 'int'.

The return statement can return one value at the maximum.

The arguments passed to the function are called as 'actual arguments'. And the arguments received by the function are called as 'formal arguments'.

The return type of library functions printf() and scanf() is an integer value. The function scanf() returns the number of arguments it reads successfully whereas printf() function returns the total number of characters it outputted on the screen.

The order in which function arguments should be evaluated is not specified in the standard.

E.g. printf("%d %d", ++n,power(2,n));

In the above expression whether 'n' is incremented first and then power() function is called or vice-versa is not fixed. Here the evaluation is compiler dependent. The GCC and Turbo-C compilers evaluated arguments in reverse order i.e. from last to first. We will discuss examples explaining this below.

† Objective Questions:

Que.3.1) Predicate the output.	**Rough work space.**

```
#include<stdio.h>
void main()
{
        int i=20;
        int j=demo(i);
        printf("%d",j);
}
int demo(int i)
{
        {
                int i=40;
}
return(i);
}
```

A.	Compiler Error
B.	Garbage
C.	40
D.	20

Que.3.2) Predicate the output.	**Rough work space.**

```
#include<stdio.h>
int i;
void main()
{
        static int j;
        int k;
        printf("%d %d %d",i,j,k);
}
```

A.	1 1 1
B.	Garbage Garbage Garbage
C.	0 0 0
D.	0 0 Garbage

Questions

Que.3.3) Predicate the output.	**Rough work space.**

#include<stdio.h>
void main()
{
static int i=2;
if(i)
{
printf("%d",i);
i--;
main();
}
}	

A.	2 1
B.	0 0
C.	2 2
D.	1 2

Que.3.4) Predicate the output.	**Rough work space.**

#include<stdio.h>
void f()
{
i=10;
printf("%d",i);
}
int i=5;
void main()
{
printf("%d",i);
f();
}	

A.	10
B.	5
C.	Compiler Error.
D.	Garbage

Que.3.5) Predicate the output.	Rough work space.

#include<stdio.h>
void main()
{
extern out;
printf("%d", out);
}
int out=100;	

A.	100
B.	0
C.	Compiler Error.
D.	Garbage

Que.3.6) Predicate the output.	Rough work space.

#include<stdio.h>
char f()
{
static char c='A';
c+=2;
return(c);
}
void main()
{
f();
printf("%c",f());
}	

A.	D
B.	A
C.	E
D.	C

Que.3.7) Predicate the output.	**Rough work space.**

```#include<stdio.h>```
```int i=0;```
```void f()```
```{```
```   i=100;```
```i++;```
```}```
```void main()```
```{```
```   i++;```
```f();```
```   i+=2;```
```f();```
```printf("%d",i);```
```}```	

A. 100	
B. 101	
C. 102	
D. Garbage	

Que.3.8) Predicate the output.	**Rough work space.**

```#include<stdio.h>```
```void main()```
```{```
```   int i=2;```
```   if(i)```
```{```
```   printf("%d",i);```
```   i--;```
```   main();```
```   }```
```}```	

A. 1 1 1 ……	
B. 2 1 0 ……	
C. 0 0 0 ……	
D. 2 2 2 ……	

Que.3.9) Predicate the output.	Rough work space.

#include<stdio.h>
int i=-3;
void f(int i)
{
i++;
printf("%d",i);
}
void main()
{
int i=2;
f(i);
printf("%d",i);
}	

A.	-3 2
B.	2 2
C.	3 2
D.	2 3

Que.3.10) Predicate the output. (Following programs are compiled and executed together)		Rough work space.

#include<stdio.h>
int i=2;
extern void f();
void f()
{
i++;
printf("%d",i);
}
	#include<stdio.h>
	extern int i;
	void main()
	{
	f();
	}	

A.	Compiler Error
B.	Garbage
C.	2
D.	3

Que.3.11) Predicate the output.	**Rough work space.**

```
#include<stdio.h>
int f()
{
static int i=-2;
return i++;
}
void main()
{
        int i,r=0;
        for(i=0;i<4;i++)
                r+=f();
        printf("%d",r);
}
```

A.	-2
B.	-3
C.	-1
D.	0

Que.3.12) Predicate the output.	**Rough work space.**

```
#include<stdio.h>
int f(int i)
{
        if(i%2)
                return f(i-1);
        return i/2;
}
void main()
{
        printf("%d",f(11));
}
```

A.	3
B.	4
C.	5
D.	6

Que.3.13) Predicate the output.

Rough work space.

```
#include<stdio.h>
int f(int n)
{
        static int s;
        if(!n)
return 0;
        s=s+n%10;
        f(n/10);
        return(s);
}
void main()
{
        printf("%d",f(1234));
}
```

A.	11
B.	10
C.	12
D.	Garbage

Que.3.14) Predicate the output.

Rough work space.

```
#include<stdio.h>
void main()
{
        int i=20;
        printf("%d %d",i,demo(i));
}
int demo(int i)
{
        i=i+100;
return(i);

}
```

A.	20 100
B.	100 20
C.	120 20
D.	20 120

Que.3.15) Predicate the output.	Rough work space.

```
#include<stdio.h>
void main()
{
        int i=20;
        int j=demo(i);
        printf("%d",j);
}
int demo(int i)
{
        i=i+100;
return(++i,200);

}
```

A.	100
B.	20
C.	120
D.	200

Que.3.16) Predicate the output.	Rough work space.

```
#include<stdio.h>
void main()
{
        int i=20;
        int j=demo(++i);
        printf("%d",j);
        j=demo(i++);
        printf("%d",j);


}
int demo(int i)
{
        i=i+100;
return(i);

}
```

A.	100 20
B.	121 20
C.	121 121
D.	121 100

Que.3.17) Predicate the output.	**Rough work space.**

#include<stdio.h>
void main()
{
int i=20;
int j=demo(i);
printf("%d",j);
}
int demo(int i)
{
i=i+100;
return(++i);
}	

A.	100
B.	120
C.	121
D.	21

Que.3.18) Predicate the output.	**Rough work space.**

#include<stdio.h>
void main()
{
int i=20;
int j=demo(i);
printf("%d",j);
}
int demo(int i)
{
i=i+100;
return(i++);
}	

A.	100
B.	21
C.	121
D.	120

Que.3.19) Predicate the output.
#include<stdio.h>
void main()
{
printf(" %d",printf("hello")*pr
intf("hi"));
}
	Rough work space.

A.	Compiler Error
B.	10
C.	hellohi
D.	hellohi 10

Que.3.20) Predicate the output.
#include<stdio.h>
void main()
{
int i=20;
int j=demo(demo(i));
printf("%d",j);
}
int demo(int i)
{
i=i*10;
return(i);
}
	Rough work space.

A.	2000
B.	Compiler Error
C.	200
D.	100

Que.3.21) Predicate the output.	**Rough work space.**

#include<stdio.h>
void main()
{
    int i;
    i=demo(10);
    printf("%d",i);
}
int demo(int i)
{
    i=i*i;
}	

A.	121
B.	200
C.	100
D.	Garbage

Que.3.22) Predicate the output.	**Rough work space.**

#include<stdio.h>
void main()
{
    int i=10;
    printf("%d",++demo(i));
}
int demo(int i)
{
    i=i*i;
    return(i);
}	

A.	Compiler Error
B.	121
C.	100
D.	Garbage

Que.3.23) Predicate the output.	Rough work space.

#include<stdio.h>
void main()
{
static int i=5;
if(--i)
{
main();
printf("%d ",i);
}
}	

A.	4 3 2 1 0
B.	0 0 0 0
C.	5 5 5 5 5
D.	0 0 0 0 0

Que. 3.24) Predicate the output.	Rough work space.

#include<stdio.h>
void main()
{
int i=i++,j=j++,k=k++;
printf("%d %d %d",i,j,k);
}	

A.	Garbage Values
B.	0 0 0
C.	1 1 1
D.	0 1 0

Que.3.25) Predicate the output.	Rough work space.

`#include<stdio.h>`
`void main()`
`{`
`    void demo()`
`    {`
`    printf("demo");`
`    }`
`    printf("main");`
`}`	

A.	demo
B.	main
C.	Compiler Error
D.	demomain

Que.3.26) How many calls are made to function f()	Rough work space.

`int f(int k)`
`{`
`    if(k>=0)`
`return 1;`
`    return f(k+1)+f(k+2);`
`}`
`void main()`
`{`
`    f(-2);`
`}`	

A.	5
B.	4
C.	6
D.	0

Que.3.27) Predicate the output.
#include<stdio.h>
void main()
{
int n=2;
printf("%d %d", ++n,
power(2,n));
}
	Rough work space.

A.	3 4
B.	3 8
C.	2 4
D.	2 8

Que.3.28) Predicate the output.
#include<stdio.h>
void main()
{
int n=2;
printf("%d %d %d",
n++,n,++n);
}
	Rough work space.

A.	3 3 3
B.	3 3 4
C.	4 3 3
D.	None of above

Que.3.29) Predicate the output.
#include<stdio.h>
void main()
{
int n=2;
printf("%d %d %d", ++n, n,
n++);
}
	Rough work space.

A.	3 3 3
B.	4 3 2
C.	4 3 3
D.	None of above

Que.3.30) Predicate the output.
#include<stdio.h>
void main()
{
int n=2;
printf("%d %d %d", n+1,
n+2,n+3);
}
	Rough work space.

A.	3 3 3
B.	3 3 4
C.	3 4 5
D.	None of above

Que.3.31) Predicate the output.
#include<stdio.h>
void main()
{
printf("HIHELLO"+5);
}
	Rough work space.

A.	LO
B.	HIHELLO
C.	HIHELLO
D.	Compiler Error

Que.3.32) Predicate the output.
#include<stdio.h>
void main()
{
show();
}
void show()
{
printf("Hello");
}
	Rough work space.

A.	Run time error
B.	No output
C.	Hello
D.	Compiler Error

Que.3.33) Predicate the output.	Rough work space.

#include<stdio.h>
void main()
{
int i;
i = abc();
printf("%d",i);
}
abc()
{
_AX = 1000;
}	

A.	Garbage
B.	1000
C.	Compiler Error
D.	0

† Answers to Objective Questions

Answer 3.1	D. 20
Explanation 3.1	In the demo() function the variable 'i' is declared twice. By applying the scope rules, the value returned from the function is 20.

Answer 3.2	D.0 0 Garbage Value
Explanation 3.2	The default value of the static and global variable is 0; whereas the default value for automatic or local variable is garbage.

Answer 3.3	A.2 1
Explanation 3.3	In the code, main() function calls itself recursively. The value of static variable 'i' is retained across the function calls. In the initial execution of main() the value 2 is printed and then value 1 is printed. The recursion terminates when 'i' becomes 0.

Answer 3.4	C. Compilation Error
Explanation 3.4	This is not the correct syntax to use external variables.

Answer 3.5	A. 100
Explanation 3.5	This is the correct syntax of using external variables inside the program. In the main() function, the variable 'out' is declared as a external variable.

Answer 3.6	C.E
Explanation 3.6	In the code, 'c' is a static variable and its value is retained across the function calls. After first call to 'f()' the value of variable 'c' becomes 'C', which later becomes 'E' after the second call.

Answer 3.7	**B.101**
Explanation 3.7	In the code, the function f() operates on the global variable 'i'. The function f() initializes value of 'i' to 100 every time.

Answer 3.8	**D.2 2 .... Infinite loop**
Explanation 3.8	Here variable 'i' is a local variable; it gets initialized to value 2 whenever main() function is called. Hence the program goes into an infinite loop.

Answer 3.9	**C.3 2**
Explanation 3.9	Apply scope rules of local and global variables.

Answer 3.10	**D.3**
Explanation 3.10	This is the correct way to call the externally defined functions and pass argument to it.

Answer 3.11	**A.-2**
Explanation 3.11	Apply properties of static variables. Note that due to post-increment used in return statement, the value of variable 'i' is returned from the function f() and then incremented.

Answer 3.12	**B.5**
Explanation 3.12	Apply recursive function call to function f(); which is as ➔ f(11) and f(10). The function call f(10) returns value 5.

Answer 3.13	**B.10**
Explanation 3.13	This is recursive program to calculate the sum of digits in a given number.

Answer 3.14	**D.20 120**
Explanation 3.14	Apply normal function execution.

Answer 3.15	D.200
Explanation 3.15	The comma operator is used in the return statement. So the return statement returns the value 200 (last value in comma operator).

Answer 3.16	C.121 121
Explanation 3.16	In the first call to demo() function pre-increment operator (++) is used in the argument. Hence value of the variable 'i' is incremented first and then passed to function demo(). Hence value 21 is passed to function. In the second call to demo() function post-increment operator (++) is used in the argument. Hence original value of the variable 'i' is passed to function and then 'i' is incremented. Here again value 21 is passed to function.

Answer 3.17	C.121
Explanation 3.17	In the return statement pre-increment (++) operator is used. Hence value of the variable 'i' is incremented first and then returned.

Answer 3.18	D.120
Explanation 3.18	In the return statement post-increment (++) operator is used. Hence the original value of variable 'i' is returned.

Answer 3.19	D.hellohi 10
Explanation 3.19	The printf() function returns number of bytes it has printed on the screen. Due to this, 10 (i.e.5*2) is displayed after printing "hellohi".

Answer 3.20	A.2000
Explanation 3.20	In the code, call to demo() function is nested. In such a case the innermost call works first which returns value 200; this value is passed as argument to outer demo() function call.

Answer 3.21	**C.100**
Explanation 3.21	In the code, the demo() function do not return any value. The result of calculation done in demo function is by default present in Accumulator register i.e. _AX. Hence the content of _AX is copied into variable 'i' and value 100 is printed.

Answer 3.22	**A.Compiler Error**
Explanation 3.22	The demo() function returns an integer value which is a constant argument for the printf() function. The compiler shows an error as it attempts to modify the constant value.

Answer 3.23	**B.0 0 0 0**
Explanation 3.23	The variable 'i' is declared as static, hence the value of variable 'i' is retained across the function calls. The main() function is called recursively until 'i' becomes 0. So after exiting recursive calls the value of static variable 'i' is printed for each function call.

Answer 3.24	**A.Garbage values.**
Explanation 3.24	The i, j and k are automatic variables and so they store garbage values as default value.

Answer 3.25	**C.Compilation Error**
Explanation 3.25	**A function can't be defined inside another function.**

Answer 3.26	**A.5**
Explanation 3.26	We can count the number of times a function is called by tracing the recursion. The following are 5 different function calls made due to recursion-: f(-2), f(-1),f(0),f(1),f(0)

Answer 3.27	**A.3 4**
Explanation 3.27	As discussed in Important Point 3.6 the GCC and Turbo C compiler evaluates arguments in reverse order; i.e. the last argument of function is evaluated first and then the second last and so on. Here power(2,n) is calculated first and then it increments value of 'n'. Note that though argument evlaution order is last to first, the order in which values are displayed depends on printf() argument ordering.

Answer 3.28	**A.3 3 3**
Explanation 3.28	Use explanation given in Answer 3.27. Also note that comma (',') operator is valid sequence point hence all side effects are made available for next expression evaluation. Hence order of evaluation is 1) ++n ➔ makes value of 'n' equal to 3 and displays it. 2) n ➔ displays and keeps value of 'n' as it is i.e. 3 3) n++ ➔ First displays value '3' and then increments 'n'.

Answer 3.29	**B.4 3 2**
Explanation 3.29	Apply the explanation given in Answer 3.28. Hence order of evaluation is 1) n++ ➔ It displays original value of 'n' i.e. 2 and then apply post increment to make value of 'n' equal to 3. 2) n ➔ keeps value of 'n' as it is i.e. 3 and displays it. 3) ++n ➔ First increments 'n' to make value '4' and displays it.

Answer 3.30	**C.3 4 5**
Explanation 3.30	Here the value of 'n' is not modified in printf() arguments ; Hence it is normal execution of function.

Answer 3.31	**A. LO**
Explanation 3.31	Due to +5, the printf() function skips the first 5 characters and then prints the rest of the string.

Answer 3.32	**D. Compiler error: Type mismatch in re-declaration of show().**
Explanation 3.32	Here the prototype of show() function is not mentioned before making function call. In such a case the compiler assumes that, 'int' is the return type of function and the function do not accepts any argument. But when the compiler sees the actual definition of show(); mismatch occurs since the return type is given as "void". Hence it gives compilation error.

Answer 3.33	**B.1000**
Explanation 3.33	The function returns the value by taking help of the accumulator register. Here _AX is the pseudo global variable denoting the accumulator. In the abc() function, the value of the accumulator is set to 1000, so the function returns value 1000.

PREPROCESSOR DIRECTIVES

Important Theory for Objective Questions:

A Preprocessor is a program that processes the code before it passes through the compiler. It operates under the control of preprocessor command lines and directives. Preprocessor directives follow the special syntax rules and begin with the symbol '#' and do not require any semicolon at the end. The preprocessor examines the source code for processing preprocessor directives before the code passes through the compiler.

These preprocessor directives extend only across a single line of code. As soon as a newline character is found, the preprocessor directive is considered to end. No semicolon (;) is expected at the end of a preprocessor directive. The only way a preprocessor directive can extend through more than one line is by preceding the newline character at the end of the line by a backslash (\).

The preprocessor directives can be divided into three categories-:

Macro substitution.

File inclusion.

Compiler control.

Sr. No.	Preprocessor Directive	Usage
1	#define `identifier` `replacement`	When the preprocessor encounters this directive, it replaces any occurrence of '`identifier`' in the rest of the code by '`replacement`'. This `replacement` can be an expression, a statement, a block or simply anything.
2	#undef identifier	The macros which are defined in the program are not affected by block structure. A macro definition is valid in the program until it is undefined with the #undef preprocessor directive.
3	#include <file-name>	When the preprocessor finds an #include directive it replaces it by the entire content of the specified file. There are two ways to specify a file to be included: #include "file" #include <file> The only difference between both expressions is the places (directories) where the compiler is going to look for the file. In the first case where the file name is specified between double-quotes, the file is searched first in the same directory that includes the file containing the directive. In case that it is not there, the compiler searches the file in the default directories where it is configured to look for the standard header files. If the file name is enclosed between angle-brackets then the file is searched directly where the compiler is configured to look for the standard header files. Therefore, standard header files are usually included in angle-brackets, while other specific header files are included using quotes.

		The C library provides several header files, each of which contains the type and macro definitions and variable and function declarations for a group of related facilities.
4	#ifdef macro-name	`#ifdef` allows a section of a program to be compiled only if the macro that is specified as the parameter has been defined, no matter which its value is.
5	#ifndef macro-name	`#ifndef` serves for the exact opposite: the code between `#ifndef` and `#endif` directives is only compiled if the specified identifier has not been previously defined.
6	#if #else #elif	The `#if`, `#else` and `#elif` (i.e., "else if") directives serve to specify some condition to be met in order for the portion of code they surround to be compiled. The condition that follows `#if` or `#elif` can only evaluate constant expressions, including macro expressions
7	#pragma	This directive is used to specify diverse options to the compiler. These options are specific for the platform and the compiler you use.
8	#error	This directive aborts the compilation process when it is found, generating a compilation error that can be specified as its parameter *#ifndef PI* *#error The constant PI is undefined* *#endif* This example aborts the compilation process and displays message "*The constant PI is undefined*" if the macro name PI is not defined.

The macro definitions accept two special operators (# and ##) in the replacement sequence. If the operator # is used before a parameter name in the replacement sequence, that parameter is replaced by a string literal (as if it were enclosed between double quotes).

```
#define mesg(x) #x
printf(mesg(Hello));
```

After preprocessing the above statement would be translated into ➔ printf("Hello");

The operator ## concatenates two arguments leaving no blank spaces between them:

```
#define concat(a,b) a ## b
concat(pr,intf)("Hello");
```

After preprocessing the above statement would be translated into ➔ printf("Hello");

The following macros are predefined: _LINE_ , _FILE_ , _DATE_ , _TIME

† Objective Questions

Que. 4.1) Predicate the output.	Rough work space.

```
#include <stdio.h>
#define MESG "Hello"
void main()
{
        printf("MESG");
}
```

A.	Run Time error
B.	Hello
C.	MESG
D.	Compiler Error

Que. 4.2) Predicate the output.	Rough work space.

```
#include <stdio.h>
#define MESG "Hello"
void main()
{
        printf(MESG);
}
```

A.	Hello
B.	MESG
C.	Compiler Error
D.	Run Time error

Que. 4.3) Predicate the output.	Rough work space.

#include <stdio.h>
#define test(a) a
#define HIGH "Hello"
void main()
{
printf("%s",test(HIGH));
}	

A.	Run Time error
B.	MESG
C.	Compiler Error
D.	Hello

Que. 4.4) Predicate the output.	Rough work space.

#include <stdio.h>
#define test(a) #a
#define HIGH "Hello"
void main()
{
printf("%s",test(HIGH));
}	

A.	Hello
B.	HIGH
C.	Compiler Error
D.	Run Time error

Que. 4.5) Predicate the output.	Rough work space.

#include <stdio.h>
#define var_a(a) a
void main()
{
int a=10;
printf("%d",var_a);
}	

A.	Compiler Error
B.	10
C.	Garbage
D.	Run Time error

Que. 4.6) Predicate the output.
#include <stdio.h>
#define test(a,b) a##b
#define HIGHLOW "Hello"
void main()
{
printf("%s",test(HIGH,LOW));
}
	Rough work space.

A.	HIGHLOW
B.	HIGH
C.	LOW
D.	Hello

Que. 4.7) Predicate the output.
#include <stdio.h>
#define g(x,y) x##y
#define f(x) x
void main()
{
printf("%d",g(f(1,2));
}
	Rough work space.

A.	12
B.	Compiler Error
C.	Garbage
D.	Run Time error

Que. 4.8) Predicate the output.
#include <stdio.h>
#define g(x,y) x##y
#define f(x) x
void main()
{
printf("%d",f(g(1,2));
}
	Rough work space.

A.	Garbage
B.	Compiler Error
C.	12
D.	Run Time error

Que. 4.9) Predicate the output.	Rough work space.

#include <stdio.h>
#define f(g1,g2) g##g2
void main()
{
int abcd=100;
printf("%d",f(ab,cd));
}	

A.	100
B.	Compiler Error
C.	Garbage
D.	abcd

Que. 4.10) Predicate the output.	Rough work space.

#include <stdio.h>
#define print_it(expr)
printf("%s:%d",#expr,(expr))
int max(int x,int y)
{
return(x>y)?x:y;
}
void main()
{
int a=10,b=20;
print_it(max(a,b));
}	

A.	20
B.	20:max(a,b)
C.	max(a,b):20
D.	max(a,b):10

Que. 4.11) Predicate the output.	**Rough work space.**

#include <stdio.h>
#define CUBE(a) a*a*a
void main()
{
    int n=2,r;
    r=64/CUBE(n);
    printf("%d",r);
}	

A.	8
B.	128
C.	Compiler Error
D.	64

Que. 4.12) Predicate the output.	**Rough work space.**

#include <stdio.h>
#define CUBE(a) (a*a*a)
void main()
{
    int n=2,r;
    r=64/CUBE(n);
    printf("%d",r);
}	

A.	64
B.	128
C.	Compiler Error
D.	8

Que. 4.13) Predicate the output.

```
#include <stdio.h>
#define CUBE(a)  (a*a*a)
void main()
{
        int n=2,r;
        r=81/CUBE(n+1);
        printf("%d",r);
}
```

Rough work space.

A.	11
B.	9
C.	Compiler Error
D.	10

Que. 4.14) Predicate the output.

```
#include <stdio.h>
#define CUBE(a)  ((a)*(a)*(a))
void main()
{
        int n=2,r;
        r=81/CUBE(n+1);
        printf("%d",r);
}
```

Rough work space.

A.	9
B.	3
C.	Compiler Error
D.	10

Que. 4.15) Predicate the output.	**Rough work space.**

```
#include <stdio.h>
#define prod(a,b) a*b
void main()
{
    int x=3,y=4;
    printf("%d",prod(x+2,y-1));
}
```

A.	12
B.	15
C.	10
D.	Garbage

Que. 4.16) Predicate the output.	**Rough work space.**

```
#include <stdio.h>
#define MAX(a,b) a<b?a:b
void main()
{
        int r;
        r=MAX(4+5+6,1+2+3);
        printf("%d",r);
}
```

A.	0
B.	1
C.	15
D.	6

Que. 4.17) Predicate the output.	**Rough work space.**

```
#include <stdio.h>
#define int char
void main()
{
    int i=65;
    printf("sizeof(i)=%d",sizeof(i));
}
```

A.	1
B.	4
C.	2
D.	65

Que. 4.18) Predicate the output.	**Rough work space.**

#include <stdio.h>
#define a 100
void main()
{
#define a 500
printf("%d",a);
}	

A.	100
B.	Garbage
C.	Compiler Error
D.	500

Que. 4.19) Predicate the output.	**Rough work space.**

#include <stdio.h>
#define getch() 100
void main()
{
clrscr();
printf("%d",getch());
getch();
}	

A.	Garbage
B.	1
C.	Compiler Error
D.	100

Que. 4.20) Predicate the output.

Rough work space.

```
#include <stdio.h>
#define FALSE -1
#define TRUE  1
#define NULL  0
void main()
{
      if(NULL)
         puts("NULL");
      else if(FALSE)
         puts("TRUE");
      else
         puts("FALSE");
 }
```

A.	TRUE
B.	FALSE
C.	NULL
D.	Compiler Error

Que. 4.21) Predicate the output.

Rough work space.

```
#include<stdio.h>
#define macro1 10
void main()
{
  #ifdef macro1
     #ifndef macro2
        printf("Hello");
     #else
        printf("Hi");
     #endif
  #endif
}
```

A.	Nothing
B.	Compiler Error
C.	Hi
D.	Hello

Que. 4.22) If we write the following statement in the program; which of the following is correct declaration of "square" macro. int s= square(2+3);		**Rough work space.**
A.	#define square(Y) (Y*Y)	
B.	#define square(Y) Y*Y	
C.	#define square(Y) ((Y)*(Y))	
D.	#define square(Y) (Y)*(Y)	

† Answers with Explanations

Answer 4.1	C. MESG
Explanation 4.1	We are using "MESG" macro here; but it does not expand as it appears as a constant string argument to printf() function.

Answer 4.2	A. Hello
Explanation 4.2	Here "MESG" macro definition replaces printf() function's argument by string "Hello".

Answer 4.3	D. Hello
Explanation 4.3	The code uses nested macros. The nested macro's expansion goes from outside to inside which is different from nested functions expansion (it goes from inner to outer). So initially "test" macro is expanded with "HIGH" as an argument; which in turns causes "HIGH" macro expansion and displays the message "Hello".

Answer 4.4	B. HIGH
Explanation 4.4	This example is the same as that of the previous with one difference viz. we use '#' symbol before argument of "test" macro. The effect of this is when "test" macro expands with "HIGH" as argument; the argument is treated as a string literal and further expansion is stopped. Hence it displays "HIGH" as output.

Answer 4.5	A. Compiler Error : Undefined symbol var_a
Explanation 4.5	Here "var_a" macro is expecting one argument which is not present in the code.

Answer 4.6	**D. Hello**
Explanation 4.6	In the code macro "test" expands initially. The "##" is used to concatenate arguments. Hence "HIGHLOW" is formed which expands to display the string "Hello".

Answer 4.7	**B. Compiler Error**
Explanation 4.7	As macro expansion goes from outer to inner; initially the preprocessor tries to expand the macro "g". The macro "g" is expecting 2 arguments which are not supplied, hence we get the error.

Answer 4.8	**C. 12**
Explanation 4.8	Here first "f" macro expands with one argument, then macro "g" is expanded to display 12 as the output.

Answer 4.9	**A. 100**
Explanation 4.9	Due to expansion of "f" macro string "abcd" is formed which is a variable name. This causes to display the value of that variable i.e. 100.

Answer 4.10	**C. max(a,b):20**
Explanation 4.10	Here "print_it" macro accepts one argument and uses that argument inside printf() function in 2 different ways. The "#expr" causes string literal replacement of the argument i.e. "max(a,b)". The (expr) causes call to max(a,b) function.

Answer 4.11	B. 128
Explanation 4.11	Here "2" becomes an argument to "CUBE" macro. The macro gets expanded as given below-: r= 64/2*2*2; In the above expression the operator "/" and "*" both have the same priority with left to right associtivity. Hence evaluation is done from left to right manner which applies "/" first; hence result is 128.

Answer 4.12	D. 8
Explanation 4.12	Here "2" becomes a argument to "CUBE" macro. The macro gets expanded as given below-: r= 64/(2*2*2); In above expression the operator "/" and "*" both have same priority with left to right associtivity. But due to parenthesis the result is 8.

Answer 4.13	A. 11

Explanation 4.13	Here "2+1" becomes an argument to "CUBE" macro. The macro gets expanded as given below-:
	r= 81/(2+1*2+1*2+1);
	By applying operator precedence and associtivity rules the resultant expression is -:
	r = 81 / (2 + 2+ 2+ 1);
	r = 81 / 7;
	Hence r = 11. (As we are dividing "integer" by "integer" the result is always an "integer".)

Answer 4.14	**B. 3**

Explanation 4.14	Here "2+1" becomes an argument to "CUBE" macro. The macro gets expanded as given below-:
	r= 81/((2+1)*(2+1)*(2+1));
	By applying operator precedence and associtivity rules the resultant expression is-:
	r = 81 / (3+3+3);
	r = 81 / 9;
	Hence r = 9.

Answer 4.15	**C. 10**
Explanation 4.15	The macro expands and evaluates as below: x+2*y-1 => x+(2*y)-1 => 10

Answer 4.16	**D. 6**
Explanation 4.16	Here 4+5+6 becomes the 1st argument and 1+2+3 becomes the second argument in the macro expansion. The macro expands and evaluates as-: r = 4+5+6<1+2+3?4+5+6:1+2+3; The operator precedence for is as -: + , -, < and then ?. Hence r = 15 < 6 ? 15 :6 r = 6.

Answer 4.17	**A. sizeof(i)=1**
Explanation 4.17	The macro replaces the string "int" by the "char". Hence "i" becomes a character variable which needs 1 byte of memory for storage.

Answer 4.18	**D. 500**
Explanation 4.18	The preprocessor directives can be redefined anywhere in the program. The most recently assigned value is taken into consideration.

Answer 4.19	**D. 100**

Explanation 4.19	The preprocessor executes as a separate pass before the execution of the compiler. So textual replacement of getch() to 100 occurs. The input program to compiler looks like this :
	`void main()`
	`{`
	`    clrscr();`
	`    printf("%d\n",100);`
	`    100;`
	`}`
	Note:100; is an executable statement but with no action. So it doesn't give any problem.

Answer 4.20	**A. TRUE**

Explanation 4.20	The input program to the compiler after processing by the preprocessor is,
	`void main(){`
	`    if(0)`
	`        puts("NULL");`
	`    else if(-1)`
	`        puts("TRUE");`
	`    else`
	`        puts("FALSE");`
	`}`
	The preprocessor doesn't replace the values given inside the double quotes. The check by if condition is boolean value false so it goes to else. In second if -1 is boolean value true hence "TRUE" is printed.

Answer 4.21	**D. Hello**
Explanation 4.21	In the code "macro1" macro is defined whereas "macro2" macro is un-defined. Hence first "ifdef" and nested "ifndef" are satisfied. Hence it displays the message "Hello".

Answer 4.22	**C. #define square(Y) ((Y)*(Y))**
Explanation 4.22	By applying the explanation given in the previous questions - we can say that only expression given in C works in all situations.

ARRAY AND POINTERS

Important Theory for Objective Questions:

A pointer is a variable which stores a memory address; this memory address may be of some other variable or even another pointer. The array is a collection of similar type of elements. The array index always starts from 0. The pointers and arrays are similar in many aspects. An array name is actually a pointer to the 0th element of the array. Dereferencing the array name will give the 0th element. This gives us a range of equivalent notations for array access. In the following examples, 'arr' is an array-:

Array Notation	Equivalent Pointer Notation
arr[0]	*arr
arr[n] OR n[arr]	*(arr+n) OR *(n+arr)
arr[i][j]	*(*(arr+i)+j)
arr[i][j][k]	*(*(*(arr+i)+j)+k)

In C Language the character array is also called as string. In C language there is no built-in data type for strings. All strings end with the NULL character('\0'). When we are passing arrays to function (i.e. array name as formal argument of function) then the base address of the array is passed to function.

The following table shows some important pointer declarations and their meanings -:

Pointer Declaration	Meaning and Usage
char str[]= "Hello World";	The 'str' is character array which stores all characters from string "Hello World" . The individual characters from 'str' can be changed but 'str' will always refer to the same memory location. E.g. str[0]='h'; // Its OK. The string becomes "hello World" ++str; /* Compiler Error: LVALUE required. 'str' is array; base address of the array can't be changed*/ str= "Bye World"; /* Compiler Error: LVALUE required. Use 'strcpy' function to copy entire new string into current string.*/
char *pstr= "Hello World";	The 'pstr' is a pointer which is pointing to a location containing the string "Hello World". E.g. pstr[0]='h'; // The string changes to "hello World". ++pstr; /* Syntactically its OK. The 'pstr' will now point to a "ello World"*/. pstr= "Bye World"; /* Its OK. The 'pstr' will now point to "Bye World" string*/.

const int *ptr;
or
int const * ptz;
	Here 'ptr' is pointer to constant integer. Hence value which is being pointed can't be changed whereas pointer can be made to point to some other data.
	
	E.g. int a = 10,b=20;
	
	const int* pcon = &a;
	
	*pcon = 20; // Error - can't change constant object.
	
	pcon=&b; // Its OK to make pointer to point to some other variable.
	
	*pcon=30; // Error. We can make the pointer to point to some other data but can't change the value.

int * const ptr;	Here 'ptr' declares a constant pointer to an integer. The location stored in the pointer cannot change i.e. we cannot change where the pointer is pointing.
	
	E.g. int a=10;
	
	int b =20;
	
	int *const ptr = &a;
	
	*ptr= 50; // Its OK to change the content of variable 'a'
	
	ptr = &b; // Error - can't change address where 'ptr' is pointing.

int **dp;	'dp' is a pointer to a integer pointer (double pointer) .
int ***tp;	'tp' is a pointer to a double pointer; this double pointer is pointing to integer.

int a[10]; int *p=&a[0];	Here 'a' is an array of size 10. And 'p' is pointer to the first element of the array i.e. a[0]. If we increment 'p' (i.e. p++) then 'p' will point to second element of the array.
int *arrp[10];	The 'arrp' is an array of 10 pointers; all these pointers are pointing to integer variables.
int (*parr)[10];	The 'parr' is a pointer to an array of 10 integers.
int (*p2arr)[2][3]	The 'p2arr' is a pointer to a 2-dimensional array; This array has 2 rows and 3 columns.
int* f();	The 'f' is a function which returns pointer to an Integer.
void *f();	The 'f'is a function which returns pointer to 'void'.
int (*pf)();	The 'pf' is pointer to a function; this function does not accept any argument and returns a integer value.
int (*f)(int (*a)[3]);	The 'f' is a pointer to function. This function accepts pointer to an array of Integers as argument and it returns an integer.

Difference between Pointers and Arrays

The concept of array is similar to the pointers. The difference between the two is that, we could change the value of pointer by another one, whereas arrays will always point to the first element of the array.

E.g.

int a[5]={1,2,3,4,5};
int *ap=a;
// as 'a' is array name it is equivalent to &a[0]
printf("%d %d", ap, *(a+0));// Arrays and pointers are similar here both displays values 1 and 1
ap++; //Its OK to increment pointer and now 'ap' points to 2nd element of the array.
a++; //Error : Its incorrect to change the base address of the array.

Pointer arithmetics

As pointers store the address; we can apply only addition and subtraction operations on pointers. But addition and subtraction have a different behavior with pointers according to the size of the data type to which they point. We will discuss this point in detail with examples given in the exercises.

'void' pointers

The `void` represents the absence of data type; hence void pointers are pointers that point to a value that has no type (and thus also an undetermined length and undetermined dereference properties). This allows void pointers to point to any data type. The data pointed by void pointers cannot be directly de-referenced; due to this we will always have to cast the address in the void pointer to some other pointer type that points to a data type before dereferencing it.

'Null' pointer

A null pointer is a regular pointer of any pointer type which has a special value that indicates that it is not pointing to any valid reference or memory address.

```
int *p;
p = 0;        //p has a null pointer value
p=NULL;       // same as above
```

The null pointer and void pointer are different. A null pointer is a value that any pointer may take to represent that it is pointing to "nowhere", while a void pointer is a special type of pointer that can point to somewhere without a specific type.

Different sizes of the pointers

The computer program memory is organized into the following segments: Data Segment (Data, BSS, and Heap), Stack, Code segment. The Data Segment stores global and static data which are initialized by the programmer. The BSS(Block Started by Symbol)segment stores all uninitialized global variables and static variables which are initialized to zero by default. The Heap segment stores dynamically memory allocated variables. The Data, BSS and Heap segments are often referred together as Data Segment. The Code segment contains machine instructions / executable computer instructions. The Stack segment contains local/

auto variables. Four registers are used to refer to four segments on the 16-bit x86 segmented memory architecture. A logical address on this platform is written as-: segment:offset.

Pointers can either be *near*, *far*, or *huge*. *Near* pointers refer to the current segment, due to this neither DS nor CS needs to be modified to dereference the pointer. They are the fastest pointers, but are limited to point to 64 kilobytes of memory (the current segment size).

The *Far* pointer stores the new value of DS or CS within them. To use them the register must be changed, the memory de-referenced, and then the register restored. They may reference up to 1 megabyte of memory. Note that pointer arithmetic (addition and subtraction) does not modify the segment portion of the pointer, only its offset. Operations which exceed the bounds of zero or 65535 (0xFFFF) will undergo modulo 64K operation just as any normal 16 bit operation.

The *Huge* pointers are essentially far pointers, but are normalized every time they are modified so that they have the highest possible segment for that address. This is very slow but allows the pointer to point to multiple segments, and allows for accurate pointer comparisons, as if the platform were a flat memory model: It forbids the aliasing of memory as described above, so two huge pointers that reference the same memory location are always equal.

Assumption -:

In the following objective questions many times we refer to memory addresses of Arrays. For simplification and understanding we will assume that the base address of the array is 0x1000. Also we will assume that 'integer' takes 2 bytes of storage also 'short' takes 2 bytes of storage. Hence if we increment an integer pointer by 1 then corresponding address will be incremented by 2.

† Objective Questions

Que.5.1) Predicate the output.	Rough work space.

#include<stdio.h>
void main()
{
int a[5]={1,2,3,4,5};
int b;
int *p=a;
b=++(*p);
printf("%d %d %d %d",a[0],a[1],*p,b);
}	

A.	2 2 2 2
B	Compiler Error
C.	Other than given options
D.	1 2 3 2

Que.5.2) Predicate the output.	Rough work space.

#include<stdio.h>
void main()
{
int a[5]={1,2,3,4,5};
int b;
int *p=&a[0];
b=(*p)++;
printf("%d %d %d %d",a[0],a[1],*p,b);
}	

A.	2 2 2 1
B	2 2 2 2
C.	Compiler Error
D.	Other than given options

Que.5.3) Predicate the output.	Rough work space.

#include<stdio.h>
void main()
{
int a[5]={1,2,3,4,5};
int b;
int *p=&a[0];
b=*(p++);
printf("%d %d %d %d",a[0],a[1],*p,b);
}	

A.	Compiler Error
B	Other than given options
C.	1 2 2 1
D.	2 2 2 1

Que.5.4) Predicate the output.	Rough work space.

#include<stdio.h>
void main()
{
int a[5]={1,2,3,4,5};
int b;
int *p=&a[0];
b=*(++p);
printf("%d %d %d %d",a[0],a[1],*p,b);
}	

A.	1 2 2 2
B	2 2 2 1
C.	Compiler Error
D.	Other than given options

Que.5.5) Predicate the output.	Rough work space.

#include<stdio.h>
void main()
{
int a[5]={1,2,3,4,5};
int i;
for(i=0;i<5;i++)
{
printf("%d",*a);
a++;
}
}	

A.	1 2 2 2 2
B	Compiler Error
C.	Other than given options
D.	1 2 3 4 5

Que.5.6) Predicate the output.	Rough work space.

#include<stdio.h>
void main()
{
int a=10;
int *p=&a;
int **dp=&p;
int ***tp=&dp;
printf("%d %d %d",*p,**dp,***tp);
printf("\n%d %d %d %d",p,dp,*dp);
printf("\n%d %d %d %d",tp,*tp,**tp);
}	

A.	Compiler Error
B	Other than given options
C.	Run time Error
D.	0 0 0 0 0 0 0 0 0

Que.5.7) Predicate the output.	Rough work space.

#include<stdio.h>
int* f()
{
int a[]={1,2,3};
return a;
}
void main()
{
int *p;
int i=1,j=1,k=1; // Dummy code
p=f();
printf("%d %d %d",i,j,k); // Dummy code
printf(" %d %d %d",p[0],p[1],p[2]);
}	

A.	1 1 1 Garbage Garbage Garbage
B	1 1 1 1 2 3
C.	Runtime Error
D.	Other than given options

Que.5.8) Predicate the output.	Rough work space.

#include<stdio.h>
char* f()
{
int char s[]="String1";
return s;
}
void main()
{
char *p="String2";
int i=1,j=1,k=1; // Dummy code
p=f();
printf("%d %d %d",i,j,k);
// Dummy code
printf(" %s",p);
}	

A.	1 1 1 Garbage Garbage Garbage
B	1 1 1 1 2 3
C.	Other than given options
D.	Runtime Error

Que.5.9) Predicate the output.

```
#include<stdio.h>
char* f()
{
char *s=" String1";
return s;
}
void main()
{
char *p=" String2";
int i=1,j=1,k=1;              // Dummy code
p=f();
printf("%d  %d  %d",i,j,k);         //
Dummy code
printf("  %s",p);
}
```

Rough work space.

A.	Compiler Error
B	Other than given options
C.	1 1 1 String1
D.	1 1 1 String2

Que.5.10)Predicate the output.

```
#include<stdio.h>
char* f()
{
static int char s[]="String1";
return s;
}
void main()
{
char *p=" String2";
int i=1,j=1,k=1;              //
Dummy code
p=f();
printf("%d  %d  %d",i,j,k);
// Dummy code
printf("%s",p);
}
```

Rough work space.

A.	1 1 1 String1
B	1 1 1 String2
C.	Compiler Error
D.	Other than given options

Que.5.11)Predicate the output.
#include<stdio.h>
void main()
{
char c[5]="Hello";
printf("%s",c);
}
	Rough work space.

A.	Compiler Error
B	Other than given options
C.	Hello
D.	Garbage content after printing "Hello"

Que.5.12)Predicate the output.

```
#include<stdio.h>
int* f()
{
        static int a[]={1,2,3};
        return a;
}
void main()
{
int *p;
int i=1,j=1,k=1;              // Dummy code
p=f();
printf("%d  %d  %d",i,j,k);         // Dummy code
printf("%d%d%d",p[0],p[1],p[2]);
}
```

Rough work space.

A.	1 1 1 3 3 3
B	Compiler Error
C.	Other than given options
D.	1 1 1 1 2 3

Que.5.13)Predicate the output.
#include<stdio.h>
int a[]={0,1,2,3,4};
void main()
{
int i,*p;
for(p=&a[0];p<=&a[4];p++)
{
printf("\n%d %d %d
",a,p,*p);
}
}
	Rough work space.

A.	Runtime Error
B	0 0 0 0
C.	Compiler Error
D.	Other than given options

Que.5.14)Predicate the output.
#include<stdio.h>
int a[]={0,1,2,3,4};
void main()
{
int i,*p;
for(p=&a[0],i=1;i<=5;i++)
printf("%d ", *(p+i));
}
	Rough work space.

A.	Compiler Error
B	Other than given options
C.	1 2 3 4 Garbage
D.	0 1 2 3 4

Que.5.15)Predicate the output.	**Rough work space.**

#include<stdio.h>
int a[]={0,1,2,3,4};
void main()
{
int i,*p;
 	
for(p=a,i=0;p+i<=a+4;p++,i++)
printf("%d ",*(p+i));
}	

A.	0 2 4
B	Compiler Error
C.	Other than given options
D.	0 1 2

Que.5.16)Predicate the output.	**Rough work space.**

#include<stdio.h>
int a[]={0,1,2,3,4};
void main()
{
int i,*p;
for(p=a+4,i=0;i<=4;i++)
{
printf("%d ", *(p-i));
}
}	

A.	0 1 2 3 4
B	4 3 2 1 0
C.	Compiler Error
D.	Other than given options

Que.5.17)Predicate the output.	**Rough work space.**

#include<stdio.h>
int a[]={0,1,2,3,4};
void main()
{
int i,*p;
for(p=a+4;p>=a;p--)
printf("%d", a[p-
a]);
}	

A.	0 1 2 3 4
B	Compiler Error
C.	Other than given options
D.	4 3 2 1 0

Que.5.18)Predicate the output.	**Rough work space.**

#include<stdio.h>
int a[]={0,1,2,3,4};
int *ap[]={a,a+1,a+2,a+3,a+4};
int **dp=ap+2;
void main()
{
printf("\n%d %d %d",
ap,*ap,**ap);
printf("\n%d %d %d",
dp,*dp,**dp);
}	

A.	Compiler Error
B	Other than given options
C.	Runtime Error
D.	0 1 2 3 4 Garbage

Que.5.19)Predicate the output.	Rough work space.

#include<stdio.h>
int a[]={0,1,2,3,4};
int *ap[]={a,a+1,a+2,a+3,a+4};
int **dp=ap+2;
void main()
{
dp++;
printf("%d %d %d", dp-ap,*dp-a,**dp);
dp++;
printf(" %d %d %d", dp-ap,*dp-a,**dp);
}	

A.	3 3 3 4 4 4
B	3 2 1 4 2 3
C.	Compiler Error
D.	Other than given options

Que.5.20)Predicate the output.	Rough work space.

#include<stdio.h>
int a[]={0,1,2,3,4};
int *ap[]={a,a+1,a+2,a+3,a+4};
int **dp=ap+2;
void main()
{
++dp;
printf("%d %d %d",dp-ap,**dp, **ap);
++**ap;
printf("%d %d %d",dp-ap,**dp,**ap);
**++dp;
printf("%d %d %d",dp-ap,**dp,**ap);
}	

A.	3 3 3 3 3 2 4 4 1
B	Compiler Error
C.	Other than given options
D.	3 3 0 3 3 1 4 4 1

Que.5.21)Predicate the output.	**Rough work space.**

#include<stdio.h>
int a[4][2]={
{1,2},
{3,4},
{5,6},
{7,8}
};
int *ap[4]={a[0],a[1],a[2],a[3]};
int *dp=a;
void main()
{
int i;
for(i=3;i>=0;i--)
printf("\n%d %d %d", a[i][i-2],*a[i],*(*(a+i)+i));
for(i=0;i<=3;i++)
printf("\n%d %d", *ap[i],dp[i]);
}	

A.	Compiler Error
B	Other than given options
C.	Runtime Error
D.	It displays content of array 'a'

Que.5.22)Predicate the output.	**Rough work space.**

#include<stdio.h>
char *c[]={"First","Second","Third","Forth"};
char **cp[]={c+1,c+2,c+3,c};
char ***cpp=cp+1;
void main()
{
printf("%s",**++cpp);
--cpp;
printf("%s",*++*cpp+3);
}	

A.	Forth th
B	Runtime Error
C.	Compiler Error
D.	Other than given options

Que.5.23)Predicate the output.
#include<stdio.h>
void main()
{
int a[]={1,2,3,4,5};
float fa[]={1,2,3,4,5};
int *p=a;
float *f=fa;
printf("%d %d %d", sizeof(a),sizeof(p), sizeof(*p));
printf(" %d %d %d", sizeof(fa),sizeof(f), sizeof(*f));
}
	Rough work space.

A.	10 2 10 20 2 20
B	10 2 2 20 2 4
C.	Compiler Error
D.	Other than given options

Que.5.24)Predicate the output.
#include<stdio.h>
void main()
{
char a[]="Hello World";
char *cp="Hello World";
printf("%d %d %d %d", sizeof(a), strlen(a), sizeof(cp), strlen(cp));
}
	Rough work space.

A.	12 10 12 11
B	Compiler Error
C.	Other than given options
D.	12 11 2 11

Que.5.25)Predicate the output.	Rough work space.

#include<stdio.h>
void main()
{
int a[4][2]={
{1,2},
{3,4},
{5,6},
{7,8}
};
int (*ap)[4];
ap=a;
printf("%d",**ap);
ap++;
printf(" %d",**ap);
}	

A.	Compiler Error
B	Other than given options
C.	1 5
D.	3 7

Que.5.26)Predicate the output.	Rough work space.

#include<stdio.h>
int a[]={0,1,2,3,4};
void main()
{
int (*ap)[5];
ap=a;
printf("%d %d", (*ap)[3],(*ap)[2]);
printf(" %d %d", *((*ap)+1),*((*ap)+2));
}	

A.	1 2 1 3
B	3 2 1 2
C.	Compiler Error
D.	Other than given options

Que.5.27)Predicate the output.	**Rough work space.**

#include<stdio.h>
void main()
{
int a[2][3]={
{1,2,3},
{4,5,6}
};
int (*ap)[1][3];
ap=a;
printf("%d %d", (*ap)[0][1],(*ap)[0][2]);
ap++;
printf(" %d %d", (*ap)[0][1],(*ap)[0][2]);
}	

A.	1 2 3 5
B	Compiler Error
C.	Other than given options
D.	2 3 5 6

Que.5.28)Predicate the output.	**Rough work space.**

#include<stdio.h>
int a[3][2]={
{1,2},
{3},
{,4}
};
void main()
{
int i,j;
for(i=0;i<3;i++)
{
for(j=0;j<2;j++)
{
printf("%d ", a[i]
[j]);
}
}
}	

A.	Compiler Error
B	Other than given options
C.	1 2 3 0 0 4
D.	1 2 3 4 0 0

Que.5.29)Predicate the output.	**Rough work space.**

#include<stdio.h>
void main()
{
int a[]={0,1,2,3,4};
printf("%d %d",*a,*(a+2));
}	

A.	0 3
B	Compiler Error
C.	Other than given options
D.	0 2

Que.5.30)Predicate the output.	**Rough work space.**

#include<stdio.h>
int a[]={1,2,3};
int* f()
{
static int i;
for(i=0;i<3;i++)
return a+i;
}
void main()
{
*f()=5;
*f()=10;
*f()=15;
printf("%d %d %d", a[0],a[1],a[2]);
}	

A.	15 2 3
B	5 10 15
C.	Compiler Error
D.	Other than given options

Que.5.31)Predicate the output.	**Rough work space.**

<code>#include<stdio.h>
int a[]={1,2,3};
int* f()
{
    static int i;
    for(;i<3;i++)
        return a+i;
}
void main()
{
    *f()=5;
    *f()=10;
    *f()=15;
printf("%d %d %d", a[0],a[1],a[2]);
}</code>	

A.	Compiler Error
B	Other than given options
C.	15 2 3
D.	5 10 15

Que.5.32)Predicate the output.	**Rough work space.**

<code>#include<stdio.h>
int a[]={1,2,3};
int* f()
{
    static int i;
    for(;i<3;)
        return a+i++;
}
void main()
{
    *f()=5;
    *f()=10;
    *f()=15;
printf("%d %d %d", a[0],a[1],a[2]);
}</code>	

A.	5 10 15
B	Compiler Error
C.	Other than given options
D.	15 2 3

Que.5.33)Predicate the output.	**Rough work space.**

#include<stdio.h>
void main()
{
int a[3][2][3]={
{
{1,2,3},
{4,5,6}
},
{
{7,8,9},
{10,11,12}
},
{
{13,14,15},
{16,17,18}
},
};
printf("%d",*(*(*(a+1))));
printf("%d",*(*(*(a+1)+1)));
printf("%d",*(*(*(a+1)+1)+1));
printf("%d", *(*(*(a+1)+1)+1) + 1);
}	

A.	7 10 13 16
B	7 10 11 12
C.	Compiler Error
D.	Other than given options

Que.5.34)Predicate the output.	**Rough work space.**

#include<stdio.h>
int a[]={1,2,3};
int* f()
{
    static int i;
return a+++i;
}
void main()
{
    *f()=5;
*f()=10;
*f()=15;
    printf("%d %d %d",a[0],a[1],a[2]);
}	

A.	Compiler Error
B	Other than given options
C.	5 10 15
D.	1 2 3

Que.5.35)Predicate the output.	**Rough work space.**

#include<stdio.h>
void main()
{
int a[3][2][3]={
{
{1,2,3},
{4,5,6}
},
{
{7,8,9},
{10,11,12}
},
{
{13,14,15},
{16,17,18}
},
};
int (*ap)[2][3];
ap=a;
ap++;
printf("%d %d",(*ap)[0][1],(*ap)[1][2]);
ap++;
printf("%d %d",(*ap)[0][1],(*ap)[1][2]);
}	

A.	8 10 12 14
B	8 12 14 18
C.	Compiler Error
D.	Other than given options

Que.5.36)Predicate the output.	Rough work space.

#include<stdio.h>
void main()
{
char x='A',y;
char *px=&x,*py;
*px=x+1;
y=*px+1;
printf("%c",y);
}	

A.	C
B	Compiler Error
C.	Other than given options
D.	Garbage

Que.5.37)Predicate the output.	Rough work space.

#include<stdio.h>
char f(char *s,char *t)
{
*s='A';
*t='B';
return *s==*t?*s:*t;
}
void main()
{
char a='X',b='Y',r;
r=f(&a,&b);
printf("%c %c %c",a,b,r);
}	

A.	X Y B
B	Compiler Error
C.	Other than given options
D.	A B B

Que.5.38)Predicate the output.	**Rough work space.**

#include<stdio.h>
void main()
{
int a[]={1,2,3,4,5,6,7,8,9,10};
int *p=&a[4];
printf("%d",p[-3]);
}	

A.	2
B	3
C.	Compiler Error
D.	Other than given options

Que.5.39)Predicate the output.	**Rough work space.**

#include<stdio.h>
void main()
{
int i;
char a[]="\0";
if(printf("%s",a))
printf("\n printf() printed some-
thing.");
else
printf("\n printf() printed noth-
ing.");
}	

A.	Compiler Error
B	Other than given options
C.	printf() printed nothing.
D.	printf() printed something.

Que.5.40)Predicate the output.	**Rough work space.**

#include<stdio.h>
void main()
{
int a[]={1,2,3,4,5,6,7,8,9,10};
int *p=a+1;
int *q=a+6;
printf("%d",q-p);
}	

A.	Compiler Error
B	Other than given options
C.	5
D.	4

Que.5.41)Predicate the output.	**Rough work space.**

#include<stdio.h>
void main()
{
char a[]="Hello\0hi";
printf("%d",strlen(a));
}	

A.	9
B	5
C.	Compiler Error
D.	Other than given options

Que.5.42)Predicate the output.	**Rough work space.**

#include<stdio.h>
void test()
{
printf("Hello");
}
void main()
{
void (*f)(void);
f=test;
(*f)();
}	

A.	Runtime Error
B	Compiler Error
C.	Other than given options
D.	Hello

Que.5.43)Predicate the output.	**Rough work space.**

#include<stdio.h>
void f(char **ca)
{
printf("%c",*(ca[2]+2));
printf("   %s",*(ca[2]+2));
}
void main()
{
char *ca[4]={"First","Second","Third"
,"Forth"};
f(ca);
}	

A.	i ird
B	i rth
C.	Compiler Error
D.	Other than given options

Que.5.44)Predicate the output.	Rough work space.

#include<stdio.h>
void f(char *ca[])
{
printf("%c",*ca[2]);
}
void main()
{
char *ca[4]={"First","Second","Third","Forth"};
f(ca);
}	

A.	Compiler Error
B	Other than given options
C.	T
D.	Third

Que.5.45)Predicate the output.	Rough work space.

#include<stdio.h>
void main()
{
int const *p=5;
printf("%d",++(*p));
}	

A.	Compiler Error
B	Other than given options
C.	6
D.	Runtime Error

Que.5.46)Predicate the output.	**Rough work space.**

#include<stdio.h>
void main()
{
char s[ ]="hello";
int i;
for(i=0;s[i];i++)
printf("%c%c%c%c ",s[i],*(s+i),*(i+s),i[s]);
}	

A.	Runtime Error
B	Compiler Error
C.	Other than given options
D.	hhhhh eeeee lllll lllll ooooo

Que.5.47)Predicate the output.	**Rough work space.**

#include<stdio.h>
void main()
{
int c[ ]={2.8,3.4,4,6.7,5};
int j,*p=c,*q=c;
for(j=0;j<5;j++)
{
printf(" %d ",*c);
++q;
}
for(j=0;j<5;j++)
{
printf(" %d ",*p);
++p;
}
}	

A.	2 2 2 2 2 2 3 4 5 6
B	2 3 4 5 6 2 3 4 5 6
C.	Compiler Error
D.	Other than given options

Que.5.48)Predicate the output.	Rough work space.

#include<stdio.h>
void main()
{
char far *f1,*f2;
printf("%d %d",sizeof(f1),sizeof(f2));
}	

A.	Compiler Error
B	2 2
C.	4 2
D.	4 4

Que.5.49)Predicate the output.	Rough work space.

#include<stdio.h>
void main()
{
char *p;
p="Hello";
printf("%c",*&*p);
}	

A.	H
B	Compiler Error
C.	Other than given options
D.	Hello

Que.5.50)Predicate the output.	Rough work space.

#include<stdio.h>
void main()
{
int *j;
{
int i=10;
j=&i;
}
printf("%d",*j);
}	

A.	0
B	10
C.	Compiler Error

D.	Garbage

Que.5.51)Predicate the output.	Rough work space.

```
#include<stdio.h>
void main()
{
        char *p;
        int *q;
        long *r;
        printf("%p  %p   %p",p,q,r);
        p++;
        q++;
        r++;
        printf("%p  %p   %p",p,q,r);
}
```

A.	Runtime Error
B	0 0 0 0 0 0
C.	Compiler Error
D.	Other than given options

Que.5.52)Predicate the output.	Rough work space.

```
#include<stdio.h>
int a[]={1,2,3};
void main()
{
        int *ptr;
        ptr=a;
        ptr+=3;
        printf("%d",*ptr);
}
```

A.	Garbage
B	Compiler Error
C.	2
D.	3

Que.5.53)Predicate the output.	Rough work space.

```
#include<stdio.h>
void fun1()
{
        printf("fun1");
}
void fun2()
{
        printf("fun2");
}
void fun3()
{
        printf("fun3");
}
void main()
{
        int (*ptr[3])();
        ptr[0]=fun1;
        ptr[1]=fun2;
        ptr[2]=fun3;
        ptr[2]();
}
```

A.	Compiler Error
B	fun1
C.	fun2
D.	fun3

Que.5.54)Predicate the output.	Rough work space.

#include<stdio.h>
void main()
{
char a[100];
a[0]='a';a[1]='b';a[2]='c';a[4]='d';
demo(a);
printf("%c",*a);
}
demo(char *a)
{
a++;
printf("%c",*a);
a++;
printf("%c",*a);
}	

A.	Bca
B	Compiler Error
C.	Other than given options
D.	Abc

Que.5.55)Predicate the output.	Rough work space.

#include<stdio.h>
void main()
{
void *v;
int a=2;
int *p=&a;
v=a;
printf("%d",(int*)*v);
}	

A.	Compiler Error
B	Other than given options
C.	2
D.	Garbage

Que.5.56)Predicate the output.
#include<stdio.h>
void main()
{
int a[5];
printf("%d",*a+1-*a+3);
}
	Rough work space.

A.	4
B	Garbage
C.	Compiler Error
D.	Other than given options

Que.5.57)Predicate the output.
#include<stdio.h>
void main()
{
char *s1="first";
char *s2="second";
strcat(s1,s2);
printf("%s",s1);
}
	Rough work space.

A.	Runtime Error
B	Compiler Error
C.	Other than given options
D.	Firstsecond

Que.5.58)Predicate the output.
#include<stdio.h>
void main()
{
char s1[20]="first";
char s2[20]="second";
strcat(s1,s2);
printf("%s",s1);
}
	Rough work space.

A.	Compiler Error
B	Other than given options
C.	Firstsecond
D.	Runtime Error

Que.5.59)Predicate the output.
#include<stdio.h>
void main()
{
char *a="hello";
a[0]='H';
printf("%s",a);
}
	Rough work space.

A.	Hello
B	Runtime Error
C.	Compiler Error
D.	Other than given options

Que.5.60)Predicate output of following code.
#include<stdio.h>
void main()
{
char a[]="hello";
a[0]='H';
printf("%s",a);
}
	Rough work space.

A.	Hello
B	Hello
C.	Compiler Error
D.	None of the above

Que.5.61)Predicate the output.	Rough work space.

#include<stdio.h>
void main()
{
char a[]="hello";
a[0]="H";
printf("%s",a);
}	

A.	Hello
B	Hello
C.	Compiler Error
D.	None of the above

Que.5.62)Predicate the output.	Rough work space.

#include<stdio.h>
void main()
{
char *s1="Hello";
if(strcmp(s1,"Hello"))
printf("Equal");
else
printf("UnEqual");
}	

A.	Equal
B	UnEqual
C.	Compiler Error
D.	None of the above

† Answers with Explanations

Answer 5.1	A. 2 2 2 2
Explanation 5.1	The array name 'a' is equivalent to &a[0]. Here 'p' is initially pointing to the first element of the array viz. a[0] or '1'. Note the operator precedenace and associtivity for '*' and pre-increment '++'. Due to ++*p the content of a[0] is incremented by 1 and it becomes 2. The value '2' is stored in 'b' due to pre-increment operator. The pointer 'p' is still pointing to a[0]. Here note that ++(*p) is equivalent to ++*p due to operator precedence and associtivity rules.

Answer 5.2	A. 2 2 2 1
Explanation 5.2	In the code, pointer 'p' is initially pointing to the first element of the array viz. a[0] or '1'. Note the operator precedenace and associtivity for '*' and post-increment '++'. Due to (*p)++ the content of 'p' i.e. a[0]=1 is assigned to 'b'. Due to post increment the pointer 'p' moves to the next element and 'p' points to a[1]. Note that (*p)++ is not equivalent to *p++ due to operator precedence and associtivity rules.

Answer 5.3	C. 1 2 2 1
Explanation 5.4	In the code, pointer 'p' is initially pointing to the first element of the array viz. a[0] or '1'. Note the operator precedenace and associtivity for '*' and post-increment '++'. Due to *(p++) the content of 'p' i.e. a[0] is assigned to 'b'. Due to post-increment operator the pointer 'p' is pointing to a[1]. Note that *(p++) is equivalent to *p++ due to operator precedence and associtivity rules.

Answers

Answer 5.4	**A. 1 2 2 2**
Explanation 5.4	In the code, pointer 'p' is initially pointing to the first element of the array viz. a[0] or '1'. Note the operator precedenace and associtivity for '*' and pre-increment '++'. Due to *(++p) the pointer moves to the 2nd location of the array i.e. a[1]. And a[1] value i.e. '2' is assigned to 'b'. Note that *(++p) is equivalent to *++p due to operator precedence and associtivity rules.

Answer 5.5	**B. Compiler Error : LAVUE required.**
Explanation 5.5	In the code, 'a' is an array and the base address of the array (i.e. &a[0]) is always fix. The statement a++ is not accepted by the compiler.

Answer 5.6	**B. Other than given option. The output is as -:** 10 10 10 Addr_a Addr_p Addr_a Addr_dp Addr_p Addr_a
Explanation 5.6	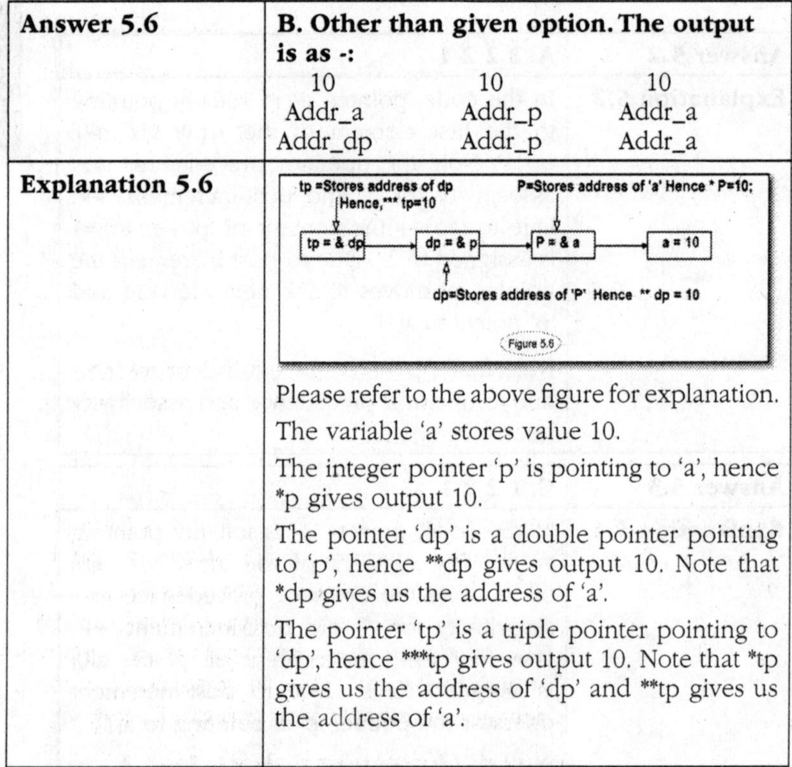 Figure 5.6 Please refer to the above figure for explanation. The variable 'a' stores value 10. The integer pointer 'p' is pointing to 'a', hence *p gives output 10. The pointer 'dp' is a double pointer pointing to 'p', hence **dp gives output 10. Note that *dp gives us the address of 'a'. The pointer 'tp' is a triple pointer pointing to 'dp', hence ***tp gives output 10. Note that *tp gives us the address of 'dp' and **tp gives us the address of 'a'.

Answer 5.7	A. 1 1 1 Garbage values
Explanation 5.7	The function f() returns the base address of array 'a'. The array 'a' is a local variable for function f(); hence the lifetime of 'a' is limited to function f(). Due to this address returned from f() no more stores same content; so we get garbage output. Please note that the dummy code (mentioned using comments) is inserted purposely. For given code certain execution environments (E.g. Turbo C on DOS environment) displays content of array 'a' as it may be present in recently used memory buffers. The dummy code is used so that buffers are filled with different content. For similar purposes in the next few examples.

Answer 5.8	A. 1 1 1 Garbage output
Explanation 5.8	The function f() returns the base address of character array 's'. The array 's' is a local variable for the function; hence the lifetime of 's' is limited to the function f().Due to this address returned from f() no more stores same content; so we get garbage output. The dummy code is inserted due to the same reason explained in above question.

Answer 5.9	A. 1 1 1 String1
Explanation 5.9	In the function f(), 's' is the pointer to a string literal. The string literal's lifetime is throughout the execution of the program; hence the content of address returned to main() remains as it is.

Answer 5.10	A. 1 1 1 String1
Explanation 5.10	In the code, function f() returns the base address of character array 's'. The array 's' is a static variable in the function f(); hence the lifetime of 's' is throughout the program. Due to this address returned from f() retains the content; so we get "C++" as output.

Answer 5.11	**D. Garbage content printed after printing string "Hello".**
Explanation 5.11	In the code, 'c' is a character array having size 5. An array of size 5 can store maximum 4 characters so that space remains for null character i.e. '\0'. The '\0' character is necessary to identify end of the string. Here array 'c' is storing 5 characters; hence end of string can't be identified. Due to this it displays garbage output after printing "Hello".

Answer 5.12	**D. 1 1 1 1 2 3**
Explanation 5.12	In the code, function f() returns the base address of character array 'a'. The array 'a' is a static variable in the function f(); hence the lifetime of 'a' is throughout the program. Due to this address returned from f() retains the content; so we get 1 2 3 as output.

Answer 5.13	**D. Other than given options. The output is as-:** **BaseAddr_a BaseAddr_a 0** **BaseAddr_a BaseAddr_a+2 1** **BaseAddr_a BaseAddr_a+4 2** **BaseAddr_a BaseAddr_a+6 3** **BaseAddr_a BaseAddr_a+8 4**
Explanation 5.13	In the code, pointer 'p' is initially pointing to base address of the array i.e. &a[0]. In the loop code it displays the following contents -: 'a' -: It displays the base address of the array i.e. & a[0] which is constant. 'p' -: It displays the address stored in pointer 'p'. Initially 'p' is storing the base address of the array; then after each iteration 'p' is incremented by 1. As 'p' is the pointer to an integer; due to p++ statement address stored in pointer 'p' is incremented by 2 (We are assuming an integer occupies 2 bytes). '*p' -: It displays content of address stored in pointer 'p'.

Answer 5.14	**C. 1 2 3 4 Garbage**
Explanation 5.14	In the code, pointer 'p' is initially pointing to the base address of the array i.e. &a[0]. In the printf() function, the value of 'i' is added to the address stored in 'p' before displaying the content. Since the initial value of 'i' is 1 it starts displaying content from a[1] and finally prints a garbage value after crossing array boundary.

Answer 5.15	**A. 0 2 4**
Explanation 5.15	In the code, pointer 'p' is initially pointing to the base address of the array i.e. &a[0]. In the printf() function the value of 'i' is added to the address stored in 'p' before displaying the content. Here both variables 'p' and 'i' both are incremented by 1 after each iteration of the loop. Hence it displays the 1st, 3rd and 5th values of the array.

Answer 5.16	**B. 4 3 2 1 0**
Explanation 5.16	In the code, pointer 'p' is initially pointing to the last address of the array i.e. &a[4]. In the printf() function value of 'i' is subtracted from the address stored in 'p' before displaying the content. Here variable 'i' content is incremented by 1 after every iteration of the loop and 'p' keeps pointing to the same element. Hence it displays array content in reverse order.

Answer 5.17	**D. 4 3 2 1 0**
Explanation 5.17	In the code, pointer 'p' is initially pointing to the last address of the array i.e. &a[4]. We can subtract one address from the other. Here base address of array i.e. 'a' is subtracted from the address stored in 'p'. Since both of these addresses are storing integer data; the result of subtraction is equivalent to the number of integer elements we can store using the addresses in the range 'p' and 'a'. This difference is initially 4. In the 'for' loop pointer 'p' is decremented by 1 after every iteration of the loop whereas 'a' keeps pointing to the same element. Hence it displays array content in reverse order.

Answer 5.18	**B. Other than given options. The output is as-:** baseaddr_ap baseaddr_a 0 Addr_dp(i.e. baseaddr_ap+4) baseaddr_a+4 2
Explanation 5.18	In the code, 'ap' is an array of pointers. The 'ap' stores addresses of an array's elements as shown in the following figure. The 'dp' is a double pointer pointing to ap[2]; which stores the address of a[2]. Also note that here we are dealing with pointers to integers. Due to this, incrementing pointer by one adds 2 to the address. Please see the following figure for explanation 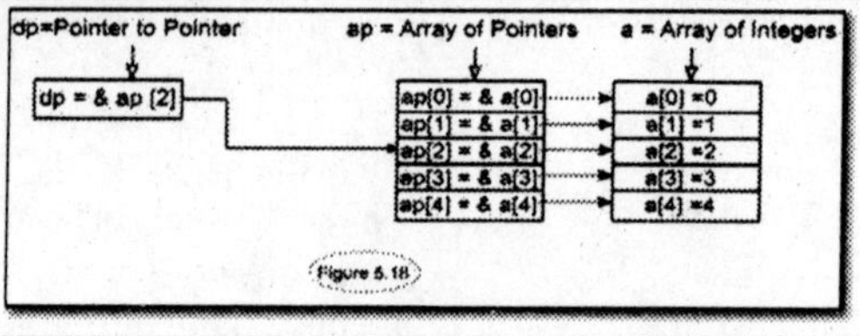 -: Figure 5.18

Answer 5.19	**A. 3 3 3 4 4 4**
Explanation 5.19	Please refer figure 5.18. After dp++ statement pointer 'dp' stores the address of ap[3]. Hence **dp displays 3. The 'dp-ap' is equivalent to &ap[3] - &ap[0]; hence the result is 3. The '*dp-a' is equivalent to &ap[3] - &a[0]; &ap[3] is storing &a[3]. Hence the expression becomes &a[3] - &a[0] which gives result 3. Similar logic can be applied to the next statements.

Answer 5.20	**D. 3 3 0 3 3 1 4 4 1**
Explanation 5.20	Please refer figure 5.18. After dp++ statement pointer 'dp' stores the address of ap[3]. 1) First printf() statement -: The 'dp' contains &ap[3]. Hence &ap[3] - &ap[0] gives result 3. The '**dp' gives content at a[3] i.e. 3. The '**ap' gives content at a[0] i.e. 0. 2) Second printf() statement -: Due to operator precedence and associtivity rules the statement '++**ap' increases content of '**ap' i.e. a[0] by 1. The other pointers remain as it is. 3) Third printf() statement -: Due to operator precedence and associtivity rules the statement '**++dp' advances pointer 'dp' by to make it point to &ap[4]. Hence 'dp-ap' is equivalent to &ap[4] - &ap[0] and gives result 4. The statement '**dp' displays content 4.

Answer 5.21	**B. Other than given options. Output is as-:** 8 7 Garbage 5 5 7 2 3 4 0 1 1 1 1 3 2 5 3 7 4
Explanation 5.21	Please refer to the figure 5.21. In the code, 'a' is a 2 dimensional array. In the statement *a[i] only one dimension is given hence the second dimension is assumed as 0. This make *a[i] equivalent to *(*(a+i)+0) OR a[i][0]. The integer pointer 'dp' stores address &a[0]. The expression dp[i] is equivalent to *(dp+i) i.e. *(&a[0]+i). Hence it displays array elements in row-wise order. dp=pointer to Integer dp = & a 'ap' = Array of Pointers a= 2 - D Array ap[0] = & a[0] ap[1] = & a[1] ap[2] = & a[2] ap[3] = & a[3] 1 2 3 4 5 6 7 8 Figure 5.21

Answer 5.22	A. Forth th
Explanation 5.22	Please see figure 5.22. In the code, statement '**++cpp' advances pointer 'cpp' by 1 to point to cp[2]; and cp[2] stores the address of c[3]; hence it displays the string "Froth". The statement '--cpp' decrements pointer 'cpp' by 1 to point to cp[1]. After applying operator precedence the statement '*++*cpp+3' can be converted into (*(++(*cpp)))+3. The '*cpp' gives cp[1]; due to ++ operator cp[1] is incremented by 1 to get pointer cp[2]. We get string "Forth" after applying *cp[2]. Due to '+3' first 3 characters from string "Forth" are skipped to display content "th". 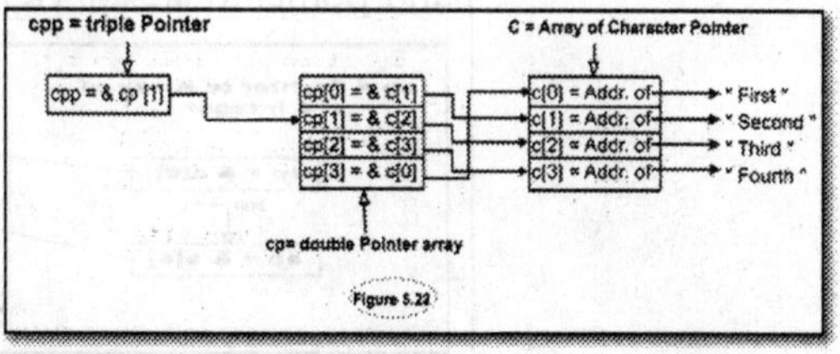 Figure 5.22

Answer 5.23	B. 10 2 2 20 2 4
Explanation 5.23	When we pass array name as argument to sizeof() function, it returns the total number of bytes occupied by the entire array. As we are assuming that the integer takes 2 bytes, the total size of 'a' is 10 and the total size of 'fa' is 20. The sizeof() of a pointer ('p' or 'f') is always fixed and is independent on the data type it is pointing. It depends on the platform. For Turbo C on DOS environment the size of the pointer is 2. The '*p' gives integer value; hence sizeof() displays value 2.The '*f' gives float value; hence sizeof() displays value 4.

Answer 5.24	**D. 12 11 2 11**
Explanation 5.24	The string "Hello World" contains 11 characters and one string terminating character (i.e. '\0'). Hence sizeof(a) gives value 12. The strlen() function gives the actual number of characters in the string; hence it displays value 11. The sizeof() a pointer is 2 as per explanation given in the above answer.

Answer 5.25	**C. 1 5**
Explanation 5.25	Please refer to the figure 5.25. In the code, 'ap' is pointer to array of 4 integers; 'ap' initially points to base address of the array i.e. &a[0]. The **ap gives value 1. After 'ap++' statement, the pointer skips the next 4 integers and points to a[2][0]. Hence **ap gives value 5. Figure 5.25

Answer 5.26	**B. 3 2 1 2**
Explanation 5.26	In the code, 'ap' is pointer to array of 5 integers. The code uses two different ways to access the elements of the array using 'ap'.

Answer 5.27	**D. 2 3 5 6**
Explanation 5.27	Apply the explanation given in the above questions.

Answer 5.28	**C. 1 2 3 0 0 4**
Explanation 5.28	Please refer the figure 5.28 to know how elements are stored in the array. a [3] [2] 1 2 3 0 0 4 Figure 5.28

Answer 5.29	**D. 0 2**
Explanation 5.29	Apply the explanation given in previous answers.

Answer 5.30	**A. 15 2 3**
Explanation 5.30	In the 'for' loop, static variable 'i' is initialized to 0 every time function f() is called.

Answer 5.31	**C. 15 2 3**
Explanation 5.31	In the 'for' loop, static variable 'i' is initialized to 0 every time function f() is called. Also due to return statement in 'for' loop code, the post-increment i++ is never executed.

Answer 5.32	**A. 5 10 15**
Explanation 5.32	Apply the explanation given in the previous answers.

Answer 5.33	**B. 7 10 11 12**
Explanation 5.33	In the code, 'a' is a 3-dimensional array. In the expression when some dimension is missing, it is assumed to be 0. Please refer to the figure 5.33. Figure 5.33 The pointers are pointing in following ways-: `*(*(*(a+1)))` ➔ a[1][0][0] ➔ 7 `*(*(*(a+1)+1))` ➔ a[1][1][0] ➔ 10 `*(*(*(a+1)+1)+1)` ➔ a[1][1][1] ➔ 11 `*(*(*(a+1)+1)+1) +1` ➔ a[1][1][1] +1 ➔ 12

Answer 5.34	**A. Complier Error : LVALUE required.**
Explanation 5.34	In the code, expression 'a+++i' is interpreted as a++ +i. The 'a' is array and 'a++' attempts to change base address of the array which is not permitted by the compiler.

Answer 5.35	**B. 8 12 14 18**
Explanation 5.35	Apply the explanation given in the previous answers.

Answer 5.36	**A. C**
Explanation 5.36	In the code, pointer 'px' is pointing to the variable 'x'. Due to statement *px=x+1 the content of variable 'x' (i.e. *px) becomes 'B'. The variable 'y' gets value *px+1 which is equivalent to 'C'.

Answer 5.37	D. A B B
Explanation 5.37	Apply the explanation given in the previous answers.

Answer 5.38	A. 2
Explanation 5.38	In the code, integer pointer 'p' is initially pointing to a[4] i.e. value 5. The expression p[-3] is equivalent to *(p-3), hence we get content which is 3 position previous to a[4] i.e. a[1]. It displays value 2.

Answer 5.39	C. printf() printed nothing.
Explanation 5.39	The printf() returns the number of characters it printed on screen. It will go on printing characters till '\0' is reached. In the code printf() does not print any character; hence printf() returns value 0. So it displays "printf() printed nothing".

Answer 5.40	C. 5
Explanation 5.40	In the code, pointer 'p' is storing the address &a[1]; whereas pointer 'q' is storing the address &a[6]. Both of these are pointers to integers. Hence 'q-p' displays the total number of integers in between 'q' and 'p'; the result is 5.

Answer 5.41	B. 5
Explanation 5.41	In the code, character array 'a' stores the initialized string, whose length is to be counted from 'H' till the null character. Here '\0' is part of the string itself; hence the result is 5.

Answer 5.42	D. Hello
Explanation 5.42	In the code, 'f' is a pointer to function which is pointing to test() function. The statement (*)(f) makes call to test() function.

Answer 5.43	**A. i ird**
Explanation 5.43	In the code, 'ca' is an array of character pointers; it is passed to function f() as argument. The expression ca[2] gives "Third" string. Adding 2 into "Third" makes pointer point to character 'i'. In the first printf() function we have used "%c" access specifer; hence it displays only one charcter 'i'. In the second printf() function we have used "%s" access specifer; hence it displays remaining string "ird".

Answer 5.44	**C. T**
Explanation 5.44	Apply the explanation given in the previous answers.

Answer 5.45	**A. Compiler error: Cannot modify a constant value.**
Explanation 5.45	In the code, 'p' is a pointer to a constant integer. The statement ++(*p) tries to change the value of the constant integer.

Answer 5.46	**D. hhhhh eeeee lllll lllll ooooo**
Explanation 5.46	The s[i], *(i+s), *(s+i), i[s] are different ways of expressing the same content.

Answer 5.47	**A.2 2 2 2 2 2 3 4 6 5**
Explanation 5.47	Apply the explanation given in the previous answers.

Answer 5.48	**C. 4 2**
Explanation 5.48	The size of a far pointer 'f1' is 4. The second pointer 'f2' is not a far pointer; hence size is 2. To make the pointer 'f2' a far pointer the declaration should be made as -: char far *f1,far *f2;

Answer 5.49	**A.H**
Explanation 5.49	The '*' is a dereference operator and '&' is a reference operator. Both operators can be applied any number of times, provided it is meaningful. Here 'p' points to the first character in the string "Hello", hence '*p' dereferences it and so gives value 'H'. Again applying '&' references it to an address and '*' dereferences it to the value 'H'.

Answer 5.50	**B.10**
Explanation 5.50	In the code, variable 'i' is a block level variable and its visibility is inside that block only. But the lifetime of 'i' is the lifetime of the main function. Hence '*j' prints the value stored in 'i' i.e. 10.

Answer 5.51	**D. Other than given options. The output is as-:** Addr_p Addr_q Addr_r Addr_p+1 Addr_q+2 Addr_r+4
Explanation 5.51	The '++' operator when applied to pointers increments address according to their corresponding data types. Hence address stored in integer pointer 'q' is incremented by 2; address stored in character pointer 'p' is incremented by 1 and address stored in long integer pointer 'r' is incremented by 4.

Answer 5.52	**A.Garbage value**
Explanation 5.52	In the code, 'ptr' pointer is pointing to an address which is out of the array's range.

Answer 5.53	**D.fun3**
Explanation 5.53	In the code, 'ptr' is array of pointers to functions; these functions have return type 'void' and do not accept any argument. The ptr[0] is assigned to address of the function fun1(). Similarly ptr[1] and ptr[2] are pointing fun2() and fun3() respectively. The ptr[2]() is in effect call to fun3().

Answer 5.54	A.bca
Explanation 5.54	Apply explanation given in the previous questions.

Answer 5.55	**A.Compiler Error. We cannot apply indirection on type void*.**
Explanation 5.55	The "void" pointer is a generic pointer type. We cannot apply indirection on the type void*.

Answer 5.56	A.4
Explanation 5.56	In the code, array 'a' is an uninitialized array; hence all elements of the array 'a' have garbage value. The '*a' and '-*a' cancels out for each other. The result is as simple as 1 + 3 = 4.

Answer 5.57	**For this question we get different answers on different program execution environments.** Turbo C in DOS Output : firstsecond GCC in Linux Output : Run time error. Here string "first" is considered as constant string and appending operation is not allowed on it.

Answer 5.58	C.firstsecond
Explanation 5.58	For both programming environments described in the above explanation we get same output.

Answer 5.59	**For this question we get different answers on different program execution environment.** Turbo C in DOS Output : Hello GCC in Linux Output : Run Time Error. Here string "Hello" is considered as a constant string and modifying the content of this string is not allowed.

Answer 5.60	**A.Hello**
Explanation 5.60	For both programming environments (described in the above explanation) we get same output.

Answer 5.61	**C.Compiler Error : Non portable pointer conversion.**
Explanation 5.61	In the code, a[0] is expecting a "character" on the right side of the expression; but a string ("H") is given. Hence it results into a compiler error. The above code works correctly if we use 'H' rather than "H".

Answer 5.62	**B.UnEqual**
Explanation 5.62	The strcmp() function returns value 0 if two strings are equal.

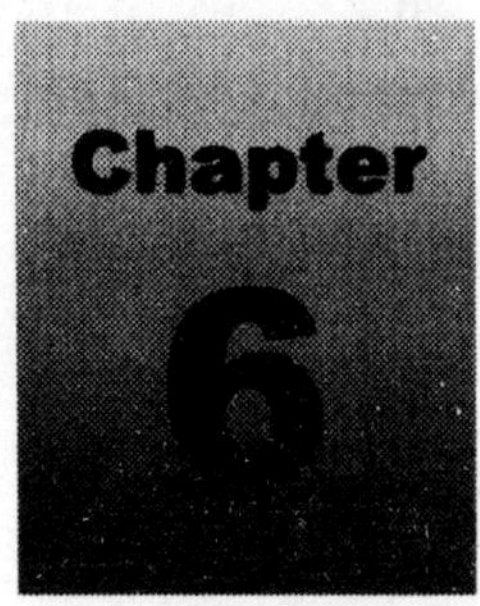

USER DEFINED DATA TYPES

Important Theory for Objective Questions:

C supports the idea of programmers creating their own data types. The structure and union are popular user defined data types; we will discuss the tricks and traps in these two data types with the help of objective questions. Other than these following are user defined data types used in C Language:

1.typedef

In C language a user can define an identifier that represents an existing data type. The user defined data type identifier can later be used to declare variables.

Syntax is-:

```
typedef datatype identifier;
```

here "datatype" represents the existing data type.

E.g. typedef int marks;

Now marks can be used to declare integer variables as ➔ marks physics, maths;

2.enum

The 'enum' is the short form of enumeration. Enumeration consists of a set of named integer constants. i.e. enumeration is a list of constant integer values.

Syntax-:

enum identifier {word1,word2,.....wordn}; OR

enum identifier { word1 = integer1, word2 = integer2,… };

If no integer values are specified then the left most word has integer value 0 and each one after that is incremented by one from that point. (0, 1, 2, 3, …)

The examples are as given below -:

Sr. No.	Example	Meaning
1	enum Boolean{ FALSE, TRUE };	The new data type (i.e. Boolean) has two values: FALSE and TRUE. The word FALSE becomes equivalent to the integer value of 0 and the word TRUE becomes equivalent to the integer value 1.
2	enum days {Mon=1,Tue,Wed,Thu,Fri};	Here a user defined data type called "days" has been defined. The new data type has five values: Mon=1, Tue=2, Wed=3 and so on.
3	enum stud {Raj,Sham=0,Ram};	The value 0 is associated with "Raj" by default. Then "Sham" is explicitly set to 0. This is allowed by some compilers whereas few do not allow it.
4	enum s1 {Raj,Sham,Ram }; enum s2 {Sita,Gita,Raj};	The code will create a compiler error as 'Raj' is declared twice.

† Objective Questions

Que. 6.1) Predicate the output.

Rough work space.

```
#include<stdio.h>
struct test
{
        int a;
        int b[3];
};
void main()
{
struct test p;
printf("%d  %d  %d
%d",p.a,p.b[0],p.b[1],p.b[2]);
}
```

A.	0 0 0 0
B.	1 1 1 1
C.	Garbage Values
D.	Compiler Error

Que. 6.2) Predicate the output.

Rough work space.

```
#include<stdio.h>
struct test
{
        static int a;
        int b[3];
};
void main()
{
struct test p;
printf("%d  %d  %d
%d",p.a,p.b[0],p.b[1],p.b[2]);
}
```

A.	0 0 0 0
B.	1 0 0 0
C.	Compiler Error
D.	Garbage Values

Que. 6.3) Predicate the output.	Rough work space.

#include<stdio.h>
struct test
{
    int a;
    int b[3];
};
void main()
{
static struct test p;
printf("%d %d %d
%d",p.a,p.b[0],p.b[1],p.b[2]);
}	

A.	Compiler Error
B.	1 1 1 1
C.	Garbage Values
D.	0 0 0 0

Que. 6.4) Predicate the output.	Rough work space.

#include<stdio.h>
struct test
{
    int a;
    int b[3];
    struct test a;
};
void main()
{
struct test p;
printf("%d %d %d
%d",p.a,p.b[0],p.b[1],p.b[2]);
}	

A.	0 0 0 0
B.	1 1 1 1
C.	Compiler Error
D.	Garbage Values

Que. 6.5) What is the right syntax to access variables 'a' and 'b' in the following code? struct test { int a; struct test1 { int b; }var1; }var;	**Rough work space.**
A.	var.a and var.var1.b
B.	var.a and var1.b
C.	var.a and var.b
D.	None of the above

Que. 6.6) What is the right syntax to access variables 'a' and 'b' in the following code? struct test { int a; struct test1 { int *b; }var1; }var;	**Rough work space.**
A.	var.a and var.b
B.	var.a and var1.b
C.	var.a and *(var.var1.b)
D.	None of the above

Que. 6.7) What is the right syntax to access variables 'a' and 'b' in the following code?	Rough work space.

```
struct test
{
        int a;
        struct test1
        {
                int b;
        }*var1;
}var;
```

A.	var.a and var.b
B.	var.a and var1.b
C.	var.a and var.var1.b
D.	var.a and var.var1->b

Que. 6.8) What is the right syntax to access variables 'a' and 'b' in the following code?	Rough work space.

```
struct test1
{
        int a;
};
struct test2
{
        int b;
};
struct test3
{
        struct test1 t1;
        struct test2 t2;
}t3;
```

A.	t3.t1.a and t3.t2.b
B.	t1.a and t2.b
C.	t3.a and t3.b
D.	None of above

Que. 6.9) Predicate the output.	**Rough work space.**

#include<stdio.h>
typedef struct test
{
int i;
int j;
}t1;
void main()
{
static t1 t;
printf("%d %d", t.i,t.j);
}	

A.	Compiler Error
B.	0 0
C.	1 1
D.	Garbage Values

Que. 6.10) Predicate the output.	**Rough work space.**

#include<stdio.h>
struct test
{
int a;
int b[3];
int *c;
};
void main()
{
struct test p={0,1,2,3,4},*q;
q=&p;
printf("%d %d %d %d",p.a,q->a, p.b[1], q->b[1],p.c,*q->c);
q->c=&q->b[2];
printf(" %d",*q->c);
++*q->c;
printf(" %d",*q->c);
}	

A.	0 0 2 2 4 4 3 4
B.	Compiler Error
C.	Garbage Values
D.	None of above

Que. 6.11) Predicate the output.	**Rough work space.**

#include<stdio.h>
struct book
{
int n;
char *bname;
};
void main()
{
struct book b={100,"java"};
struct book *p=&b;
printf("%s %c",p->bname, *p-
>bname);
printf(" %c",*p->bname++);
}	

A.	Compiler Error
B.	java j j
C.	Run time error
D.	None of above

Que. 6.12) Predicate the output.	**Rough work space.**

#include<stdio.h>
struct test
{
int a;
float b;
char c[3];
double e[2];
};
void main()
{
printf("%d",sizeof(struct test));
}	

A.	16
B.	17
C.	25
D.	None of above

Que. 6.13) Predicate the output.	**Rough work space.**

#include<stdio.h>
union test
{
int a;
float b;
char c[3];
double e[2];
};
void main()
{
printf("%d",sizeof(union test));
}	

A.	18
B.	17
C.	25
D.	16

Que. 6.14) Predicate the output.	**Rough work space.**

#include<stdio.h>
union test
{
int a;
float f;
};
void main()
{
union test t={2.3};
printf("%d %f",t.a,t.f);
}	

A.	Compiler Error
B.	2.3 0
C.	2 0.00
D.	0 2.3

Que. 6.15) Predicate the output.	Rough work space.

#include<stdio.h>
union test
{
int a;
float f;
};
void main()
{
union test t={2,2.3};
printf("%d %f",t.a,t.f);
}	

```
#include<stdio.h>
union test
{
        int a;
        float f;
};
void main()
{
        union test t={2,2.3};
printf("%d   %f",t.a,t.f);
}
```

A.	Compiler Error
B.	2.3 0
C.	2 0.00
D.	0 2.3

Que. 6.16) Predicate the output. | **Rough work space.**

```
#include<stdio.h>
union test
{
        int a;
        float f;
};
void main()
{
        union test t;
t.a=2;
t.f=2.3;
printf("%d   %f",t.a,t.f);
}
```

A.	Compiler Error
B.	Garbage 2.3
C.	2 0.00
D.	0 2.3

Que. 6.17) What is the right syntax to access variables 'a' and 'b' in the following code? union test { int a; struct test1 { int b; }t1; }t2;	**Rough work space.**
A.	t2.a and t2.t1.b
B.	t2.a and t2.b
C.	t1.a and t1.b
D.	None of above

Que. 6.18) Predicate the output.
#include<stdio.h>
struct test
{
char *a;
int b;
struct test *next;
};
struct test s[]={
{"abc",1,s+2},
{"def",2,s+1},
{"ghi",0,s}
};
void main()
{
struct test *p=s;
printf("%s",s[(p++)->b].a);
printf("%s",s[p->b].a);
printf("%c",(s[p->b].a)[2]);
}
	Rough work space.

A.	def ghi ghi
B.	d g i
C.	def ghi i
D.	Compiler Error

Que. 6.19) Predicate the output.	Rough work space.

#include<stdio.h>
struct xx
{
int x=3;
char name[]="hello";
 };
void main()
{
struct xx *s;
printf("%d",s->x);
printf("%s",s->name);
}	

A.	3 hello
B.	3 Garbage
C.	Garbage 3
D.	Compiler Error

Que. 6.20) Predicate the output.	Rough work space.

#include<stdio.h>
 struct position
{
int x;
int y;
int z;
 };
struct position p1;
struct position *p2;
void main()
{
p2=&p1;
printf("%d %d %d",p1.x,p1.y,p1.z);
printf(" %d %d
%d",(*p2).x,(*p2).y,(*p2).z);
printf(" %d %d %d",p2->x,p2->y,p2-
>z);
}	

A.	0 0 0 0 0 0 0 0 0
B.	Garbage values
C.	Compiler Error
D.	None of above

Que. 6.21) Predicate the output.	Rough work space.

#include<stdio.h>
enum colors {Mon,Tue,Wed};
void main()
{
printf("%d %d %d", Mon,Tue,Wed);
}	

A.	Compiler Error
B.	Garbage Values
C.	1 2 3
D.	0 1 2

Que. 6.22) Predicate the output.	Rough work space.

#include<stdio.h>
void main()
{
enum month{Jan, Feb=3,
Mar,Apr=8,May};
printf("%d %d %d %d", Jan, Feb,
Mar, May);
}	

A.	0 3 4 9
B.	2 3 4 9
C.	0 3 4 5
D.	None of above.

† Answers with Explanations:

Answer 6.1	C. Garbage values
Explanation 6.1	The storage classes are applicable to structure variables. In the code 'p' is the local structure variable; hence default values for structure members are garbage values.

Answer 6.2	C. Compiler Error: Storage class static not allowed in structure declaration.
Explanation 6.2	The storage classes are applicable to the structure variable (E.g. 'p') and not for the structure members (E.g. 'static int a'). In the code an attempt is made to use static structure member which is not permitted.

Answer 6.3	D. 0 0 0 0
Explanation 6.3	The storage classes are applicable to structure variables. In the code 'p' is a static variable; hence default values for structure members are 0's.

Answer 6.4	C. Compiler Error : Undefined structure test.

Explanation 6.4	The structure declaration ends with a semi colon. Hence declaring a structure variable inside the structure declaration is not permitted.
	
	But note that, we can declare a self referential structure inside the structure declaration. The following code explains the same -:
	
	E.g. struct test
	{
	    int a;
	    struct test p1; // Wrong syntax
	    struct test *p2; // Correct syntax – self referential structure
	}

Answer 6.5	**A. var.a and var.var1.b**
Explanation 6.5	The 'test1' structure is declared inside the structure 'test'. The members of inner structure are accesses by using the syntax as ➔ var. var1.b.

Answer 6.6	**C. var.a and *(var.var1.b)**
Explanation 6.6	The 'test1' structure is declared inside the structure 'test'. The strcture member 'b' is a pointer to an integer; hence dereference ('*') operator is used to access the content. Hence correct syntax is ➔ *(var.var1.b) Please note that in addition to the above syntax, certain compilers (E.g. TurboC) permits a different syntax as well ➔ var. var1.b.

Answer 6.7	**D. var.a and var.var1->b**
Explanation 6.7	The 'test1' structure is declared inside the structure 'test'. Also note that 'var1' is a structure pointer and hence we need to use -> operator to access the data member. Hence correct syntax to access variable 'b' is ➔ var. var1->b.

Answer 6.8	**A. t3.t1.a and t3.t2.b**
Explanation 6.8	Apply the explanation given in the above answers.

Answer 6.9	**B. 0 0**
Explanation 6.9	In the code a new data type 't1' is created with the help of 'typedef'. Then a static variable 't' is created which has default value 0 for the data members of the structure.

Answer 6.10	**A. 0 0 2 2 4 4 3 4**
Explanation 6.10	Explanation 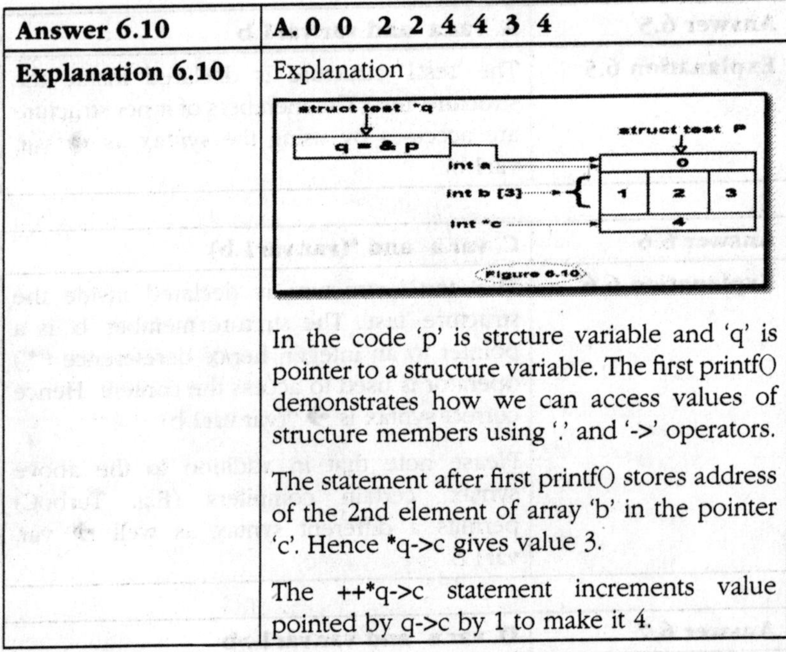 Figure 6.10 In the code 'p' is strcture variable and 'q' is pointer to a structure variable. The first printf() demonstrates how we can access values of structure members using '.' and '->' operators. The statement after first printf() stores address of the 2nd element of array 'b' in the pointer 'c'. Hence *q->c gives value 3. The ++*q->c statement increments value pointed by q->c by 1 to make it 4.

Answer 6.11	**B. java j j**
Explanation 6.11	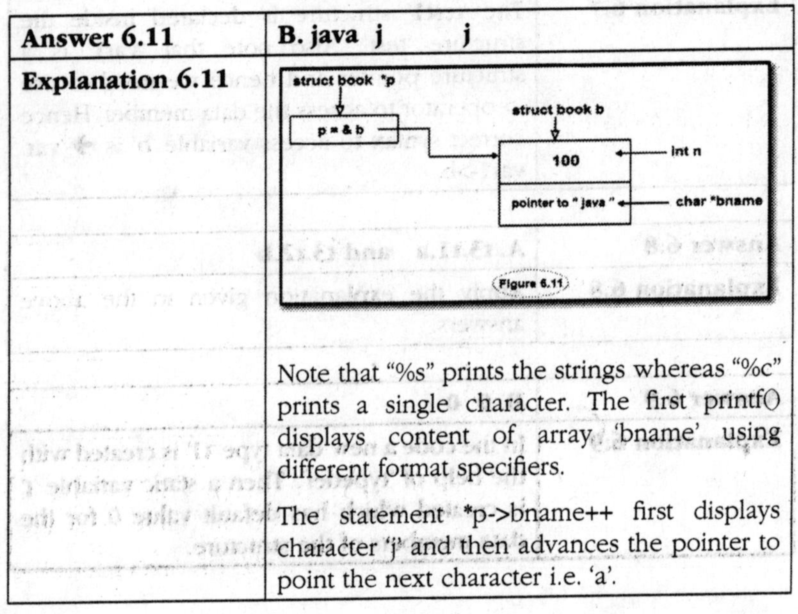 Figure 6.11 Note that "%s" prints the strings whereas "%c" prints a single character. The first printf() displays content of array 'bname' using different format specifiers. The statement *p->bname++ first displays character 'j' and then advances the pointer to point the next character i.e. 'a'.

Answer 6.12	**C. 25**
Explanation 6.12	The structure elements are always stored in adjacent memory locations. The memory is allocated after creation of the structure variable and not after declaration of the structure. But 'sizeof' function estimates the amount of memory required depending on structure data members. In this case it is -: 2 Bytes (int a) + 4 Bytes (float b) + 3 Bytes (char c[3]) + 16 Bytes (double e[2]) = 25 Bytes.

Answer 6.13	**D. 16**
Explanation 6.13	The memory allocation for a union variable is different that a structure variable. The memory allocated for a union variable memory is equal to maximum memory needed to store any union member. Here 'e' is the double array of size 2; hence memory requirement is 16 Bytes.

Answer 6.14	**C. 2 0.00**
Explanation 6.14	In the union, we can store value for only one member at one time. The value 2.3 goes to member 'a' which is an integer; hence it stores the value 2. The member 'f' has the value 0.0.

Answer 6.15	**A. Compiler Error**
Explanation 6.15	As mentioned in the above explanation, in the union we can have value for one member at one time. Hence the given code does not get compiled as it is attempted to initialize values for two members. Please note that, the code given in 6.15 is different than code in 6.14.

Answer 6.16	**B. Garbage 2.3**
Explanation 6.16	Here initially member 'a' gets value 2 but afterwards member 'f' gets the value 2.3. Hence when we try to access member 'a' it shows garbage value.

Answer 6.17	**A. t2.a and t2.t1.b**
Explanation 6.17	Apply the same explanation as discussed for structure.

Answer 6.18	**C. def ghi i**
Explanation 6.18	This code uses self referential strctures. The following figure explains how self referential strcture is pointing to other variable. Figure 6.18 The 'test' is a self referential structure wherein one of the structure member is pointer to similar structure variable. The pointer 'p' is initially pointing to structure variable s[0]. The following is the way code executes -: 1) s[(p++)->b].a (p++)->b gives value 1. Hence s[1].a is "def". Afterwards pointer 'p' is advanced to point s[1]. 2) s[p->b].a As pointer is pointing to s[1]; p->b gives value 2. Hence s[2].a displays "ghi". 3) (s[p->b].a)[2] As above p->b gives value 2. Hence s[2].a is pointing to "ghi". Due to index 2 only 3rd character i.e. 'i' is displayed.

Answer 6.19	D. Compiler Error
Explanation 6.19	The compiler does not allow initialization of the structure members in the declaration.

Answer 6.20	A. 0 0 0 0 0 0 0 0 0
Explanation 6.20	The structure variable 'p1' is globally declared; hence 'x', 'y' and 'z' are initialized with zeroes. The 'p2' is a pointer to structure variable 'p1'. We can access the elements of the structure either with an arrow mark ('->') or with indirection operator ('*').

Answer 6.21	D. 0 1 2
Explanation 6.21	The enum assigns numbers starting from 0, if not explicitly defined.

Answer 6.22	A. 0 3 4 9
Explanation 6.22	The 'Jan' gets default value i.e. 0. As 'Feb' is assigned value 3; the next member 'Mar' gets value 4. In a similar way 'May' gets value 9.

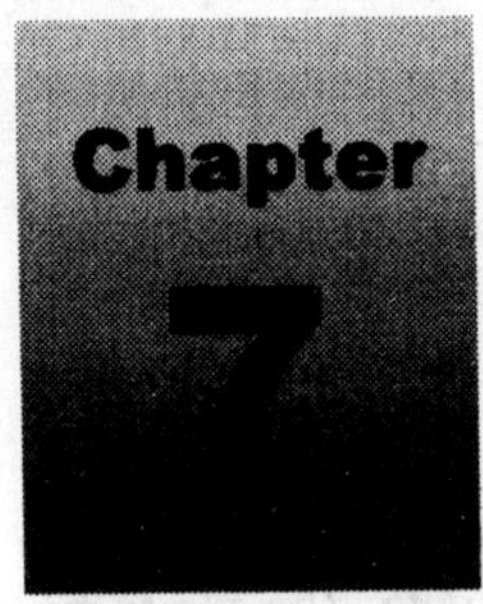

FILE HANDLING

Important Theory for Objective Questions:

A file is a place on the disk where a group of related data is stored. Following different operations can be carried out on a file -: Creation of a new file, Opening an existing file, Reading from a file, Writing to a file, Moving to a specific location in a file, Closing a file.

A file must be opened before any I/O operations can be performed on that file. The "fopen" function is used to open a file.

Declaration: FILE *fopen (const char *filename, const char *mode);

The second argument is the mode that decides which operations (read, write, append) can be performed on the file. The fopen() returns a FILE pointer on successful opening of file and returns NULL on error. The possible values of modes are given below -:

1) "w" (write)

If the file does not exist then this mode creates a new file for writing, and if the file already exists then the previous data is erased and the new data is written to the file.

2) "a" (append)

If the file does not exist then this mode creates a new file, and if the file already exists then the new data entered is appended at the end of the existing data. In this mode data existing in the file is not erased.

3) "r" (read)

This mode is used for opening an existing file for reading purpose only. The file to be opened must exist. In this mode the previous data of the file is not erased.

4) "w+"

In this mode we can read and modify data from the file. If the file does not exist then a new file is created, and if the file exists then previous data is erased.

5)"r+"

This mode is same as "r" mode, with the difference that in this mode we can also write and modify existing data. The file to be opened must exist and previous data of the file is not erased.

6) "a+"

This mode is same as "a" mode with the difference that in this mode we can also read the data stored in the file. If the file does not exist, a new file is created and the file already exists the new data is appended at the end of existing data. We cannot modify existing data in this mode.

To open a file in a binary mode you must add a "b" to the end of the mode string; for example, "rb" for the reading and to have reading and writing modes you can add if "b" either after the plus sign (like "r+b") or before plus sign (like "rb+").

The following functions are used for file Input Output operations -:

1) Character I/O - These functions are used to read or write one character at a time. E.g. fgetc(), fputc().

2) String I/O – These functions are used for reading or writing entire lines of data from and to a file. E.g. fgets(), fputs().

3) Formatted I/O - These functions are used for reading and writing data from and to the file in formatted way. E.g. fscanf(), fprintf().

4) Record OR Block I/O - These functions are used for reading or writing an entire block or record to a given file. E.g. fread(), fwrite().

The data stored in the file can be accessed in two ways-: Sequentially, Randomly. If we want to access a particular record from the file then random access takes less time than sequential access.

Following three functions are used for random access to file.

1. fseek()

Declaration: int fseek (FILE * fp, long displacement, int origin);

This function is used for setting the file position pointer at the specified bytes. Here the "fp" is a file pointer. The "displacement" is a long integer which can be positive or negative, it denotes the number of bytes which are skipped backward (if negative) or forward (if positive) from the position specified in the third argument. The third argument "origin" is the position related to which the displacement takes place. It can be one of following three values -:

Constants	**Value**	**Position**
SEEK_SET	0	Beginning of the file
SEEK_CUR	1	Current position
SEEK_END	2	End of the file

E.g. i) fseek(p,10,0): The pointer position is moved 10 bytes forward from the beginning of the file.

ii) fseek(p,-3,1): The pointer position is moved 3 bytes backward from the current position in the file.

2. ftell()- The function returns the current position of the file position pointer. The value is counted from the beginning of the file.
Declaration: long ftell(FILE *fp);

3. rewind() - This function is used to move the file position pointer to the beginning of the file.
Declaration: void rewind(FILE *fp);

Important Points-:

The file that is opened using "fopen" must be closed if there are no more operations to be performed on the file. After closing the file, connection between file and program is broken.

If "fopen" fails to open file due to some reason then "fopen" will return 0 (NULL pointer).

"fclose" returns zero value if the file is closed successfully.

A structure named "FILE" is declared in "stdio.h" that contains all the information about the file. Note that "FILE" is a data type name like "int".

The EOF is a constant defined in the file "stdio.h" and its value is -1. The EOF represents the end of the file.

The "fflush()" function flush any buffered output associated with the file. If the given stream was open for writing and the last i/o operation was an output operation, using call to "fflush" function it is ensured that any unwritten data in the output buffer is written to the file.

When C program execution starts the operating system automatically opens three files and provides file pointers to them. These files are standard input, standard output, and standard error. The corresponding file pointers are – stdin, stdout, stderr ; these are declared in "stdio.h" header file. Normally stdin is connected to keyboard, stdout and stderr are connected to monitor.

† Objective Questions

Que. 7.1) What does the pointer “fp” point to in the following program?	**Rough work space.**

```
#include<stdio.h>
int main()
{
FILE *fp;
fp=fopen("file1.txt", "r");
fclose(fp);
return 0;
}
```

A.	The first character in the file.
B.	A structure which contains information about the file.
C.	The name of the file.
D.	The last character in the file.

Que. 7.2) Predicate the output of following program.	Rough work space.

#include<stdio.h>
#include<conio.h>
void main()
{
FILE *fp;
char ch, str[20];
int res,pos;
fp=fopen("file1.txt", "rw");
fputs(fp,"India is great");
fseek(fp, 7, SEEK_CUR);
ch = fgetc(fp);
printf("%c",ch);
fseek(fp, -4, SEEK_CUR);
ch = fgetc(fp);
printf("%c",ch);
pos=ftell(fp);
printf("%d",pos);
fclose(fp);
}	

A.	s a 5
B.	i a 4
C.	s a 4
D.	i i 4

Que. 7.3) Predicate the output of following program.	Rough work space.

#include<stdio.h>
void main()
{
FILE *fp;
char ch, str[20];
int res,pos;
clrscr();
fp=fopen("file1.txt","rw");
fputs(fp,"india is great");
fseek(fp, 0, SEEK_SET);
ch = fgetc(fp);
printf("%c",ch);
pos=ftell(fp);
printf("%d",pos);
fseek(fp, 3, SEEK_CUR);
ch = fgetc(fp);
printf("%c",ch);
pos=ftell(fp);
printf("%d",pos);
fclose(fp);
}	

A.	i 2 a 5
B.	i 1 a 6
C.	i 1 a 5
D.	i 2 a 6

Que. 7.4) Predicate the output of following program.
#include<stdio.h>
int main()
{
unsigned char ch;
FILE *fp;
fp=fopen("file1.txt", "r");
while((ch = getc(fp))!=EOF)
printf("%c", ch);
fclose(fp);
return 0;
}
	Rough work space.

A.	Compiler Error
B.	Linker Error
C.	Infinite loop
D.	It displays content of the file "file1.txt"

Que.7.5) Predicate the output of following program.
#include<stdio.h>
int main()
{
char ch;
FILE *fp;
fp=fopen("file1.txt", "r");
while((ch = getc(fp))!=EOF)
printf("%c", ch);
fclose(fp);
return 0;
}
	Rough work space.

A.	Compiler Error
B.	Linker Error
C.	Infinite loop
D.	It displays content of the file "file1.txt"

Que. 7.6) Predicate what will be content of the file "file2.txt" after execution of the program.	**Rough work space.**

```
#include<stdio.h>
int main()
{
int i;
char ch;
FILE *f1 = fopen("file1.txt","r"); /* file
contains string "India is great" */
FILE *f2 = fopen("file2.txt", "w");
while(1)
{
        ch=getc(f1);
        if(ch==EOF)
                break;
        fseek(f1, 2, SEEK_CUR);
        fputc(ch, f2);

}
fclose(f1);
fclose(f2);
return 0;
}
```

A.	I i i g a
B.	India is great
C.	India
D.	Run time error

† Answers with Explanations:

Answer 7.1	**B. A structure which contains information about the file.**
Explanation 7.1	The "fp" pointer points to a structure that contains information about the file. This information includes whether file is being read or written, whether error or EOF has occurred, location of buffer, current character position in the buffer etc.

Answer 7.2	**A. s a 5**
Explanation 7.2	Here "file1.txt" is opened in read / write mode. The string "India is great" is written to file using fputs() function. At this moment read pointer is pointing to 0th position in the file i.e. first character. Due to statement "fseek(fp, 7, SEEK_CUR)" the pointer is moved 7 position in forward direction. At this point of time the pointer is pointing to 8th character i.e. 's'. Hence fgetc() functions reads character 's' and moves read pointer one position in forward direction. Now pointer is pointing to the 9th character i.e. blank space (' '). Due to statement "fseek(fp, -4, SEEK_CUR)" the pointer is moved 4 position in backward direction. At this point of time the pointer is pointing to 5th character which is 'a'. Again due to fgetc() pointer moves one position further making it point to 6th character. Now when we try to get the position of pointer it gives us the result value 5.

Answer 7.3	**C. i 1 a 5**
Explanation 7.3	Please refer explanation given for question 7.2.

Answer 7.4	**C. Infinite loop**
Explanation 7.4	The value of "EOF" is -1; which is a signed integer. As variable 'ch' is declared as "unsigned char" it cannot deal with any negative value. Hence comparison in if condition is always TRUE which causes infinite loop after displaying the content of the file.

Answer 7.5	**D. It displays content of the file "file1.txt"**
Explanation 7.5	Please refer explanation given for question 7.4. Note that for variable 'ch' the default data type is signed character.

Answer 7.6	**A. I i i g a**
Explanation 7.6	The program writes first character i.e. 'I' to the output file. Then onwards every time it skips next 2 characters and writes next character to the output file.

MISCELLANEOUS QUESTIONS

Important Theory for Objective Questions:

In this chapter we will discuss the Dynamic memory allocation, Command line arguments, Bit fields, Automatic type conversions, Operator restrictions and few other miscellaneous concepts.

A) Dynamic Memory Allocation

The C language supports following three types of memory allocation:

1) Static allocation

The Static memory allocation is done for static or global variables. The space is allocated when program is starts the execution and freed after termination of the program.

2) Automatic allocation

The Automatic memory allocation is done for automatic or local variables. The space is allocated when an automatic variable is declared in function or block; the space is freed when the respective block of code or function terminates.

3) Dynamic allocation

The Dynamic memory allocation is needed when it's not possible to predicate the amount of memory needed for storing the data. The Dynamic allocation is not supported by C variables; system calls are needed for dynamic memory allocation. The process of dynamic allocation requires more computation time compared to the static memory allocation.

Following functions are used for dynamic memory allocations and de-allocations. These functions are declared in stdlib.h header file.

malloc() – It allocates the specified number of bytes of memory as per requirements.

realloc() – It increases the size of the specified block of memory; also relocates the memory if needed.

calloc() – It allocates the specified number of bytes and initializes them to zero.

free() - It releases the specified block of memory back to the system.

The improper use of dynamic memory allocation can frequently be a source of bugs. The most common errors are as follows:

1) Allocation failure -: The memory allocation is not guaranteed after making calls to malloc() or calloc() functions. The return value of these functions may be NULL if system does not find sufficient memory for the allocation. If there's no check for successful allocation implemented, this usually leads to a crash of the program.

2) Memory leaks -: It is needed to de-allocate the dynamically allocated memory after it usage are over. This has to be done by making explicit call to free() function. Failure to de-allocate memory using free() leads to non-reusable memory. This wastes memory resources and may cause allocation failures when the memory resources are exhausted.

3) Logical errors -: The memory allocations must follow the sequence of actions as -: allocation using malloc() or calloc() , usage of the data, and lastly de-allocation using free(). If this sequence is not followed it leads to logical errors and may causes crash of the program. E.g. memory usage after call to a free or before call to malloc, calling free twice, etc. usually leads to a crash of the program.

B) Command Line Arguments

The C language provides a method to pass parameters to the main() function. This is typically accomplished by specifying arguments on the operating system command line (console). The prototype for main() looks like ➔ int main(int argc, char *argv[]).

The first parameter is the number of items on the command line (int argc). The second parameter passed to main() is an array of pointers to the character strings containing each argument (char *argv[]).

E.g. If you type following at the command prompt:

myprog hello 1 hi 2

There are 5 items on the command line, so the operating system will set argc=5. The parameter argv is a pointer to an array of pointers to strings of characters, such that:

argv[0] is a pointer to the string "myprog"
argv[1] is a pointer to the string "hello"
argv[2] is a pointer to the string "1"
argv[3] is a pointer to the string "hi"
argv[4] is a pointer to the string "2"

C) Bit Fields

The combination of pointers and bit-level operators makes C useful for many low level applications. The Bit Fields allow the packing of data in a structure. This is especially useful when memory resource has to be utilized with utmost care to avoid wastage. The C langauge permit us to put bit length after the variable; this is shown in below example.

```
struct bfld {
        unsigned int f1:2;
        unsigned int f2:2;
        unsigned int f3:1;
        unsigned int f4:2;
        unsigned int type:4;
        unsigned int funny_int:6;
} b1;
```

Here the "bfld" contains 6 members; flag f1 requires 2 bits, flag f3 requires 1 bit and so on. Access members as usual via-: b1.type = 7;

NOTE:

1. If we are allocating 'n' bits for a variable then maximum value for that

variable can be 2^n-1 (OR 2^n-1).

2. The Bit fields are always converted to integer type for computation.

3. It is allowed to mix normal data types with bit fields in structure definitions.

4. The Bit fields do suffer from a lack of portability between platforms.

D) Automatic type conversions

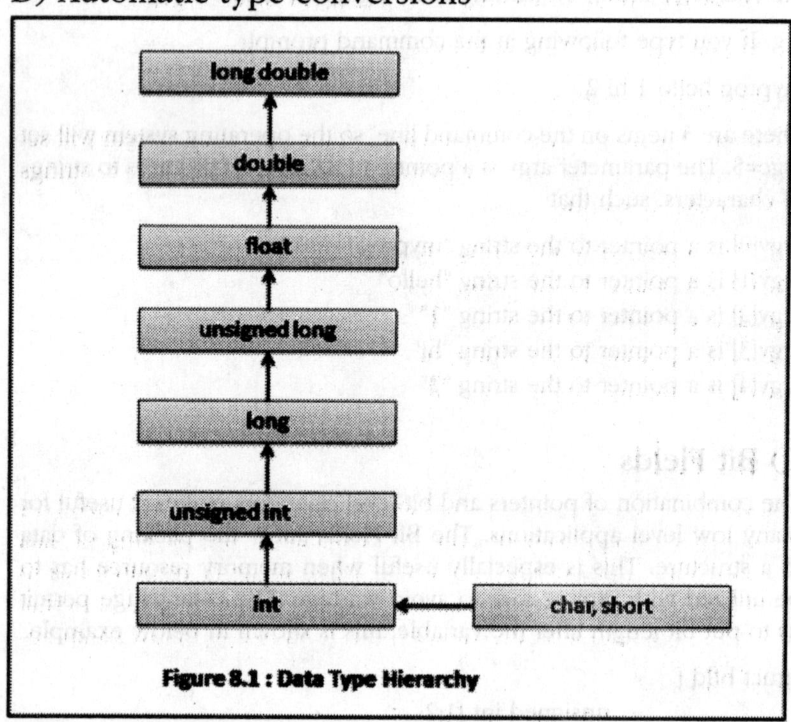

Figure 8.1 : Data Type Hierarchy

In the above figure vertical arrows indicates basic ordering of the data types; e.g. "long" is having higher ordering than "int". During the evaluation of a binary operator initially it is ensured that both operands are of similar data type. If operands are of different data types then the operand with lower ordering (as per figure) is converted into data type of higher ordering operand. The horizontal arrow indicates the automatic type conversions. E.g. operands of type "char" or "short" are always converted into type "int" before applying the operator.

Sometimes width and precision is included in printf() statement. The printf() processes width and precision in following ways -:

- %d = Prints data as a decimal integer

- %6d = Prints data as a decimal integer with a width of at least 6 wide
- %f = Prints data as a floating point
- %4f = Prints data as a floating point with a width of at least 4 wide
- %.4f = Prints data as a floating point with a precision of four characters after the decimal point
- %3.2f = Prints data as a floating point at least 3 wide and a precision of 2

E) Operator Restrictions

We have discussed operators in previous chapters. The operators in C language have to be used with some restrictions to avoid compile and run time errors. Following table summarizes restrictions on different operators from C language.

Sr. No.	Operator	Restriction	Example
1	Arithmetic '+' E.g. a+b	If one operand (either 'a' or 'b') is a pointer then other operand must be an integral.	If 'p' and 'q' are pointers then p+3 ➔ Allowed p+q ➔ Not allowed
2	Arithmetic '-' E.g. a-b	If one operand (either 'a' or 'b') is a pointer then other operand must be an integral or a pointer of the same base type.	If 'p' & 'q' are pointers then p-3 ➔ Allowed p-q Allowed if p & q are pointing to similar type of data.
3	Multiplication '*' Division '/' E.g. a*b or a/b	Here 'a' and 'b' cannot be pointers.	If 'p' is pointer then p*3 ➔ Not allowed 300/p ➔ Not allowed
4	Modulo '%' E.g. a%b	Here 'a' and 'b' cannot be double, float or pointers.	If 'd' is double then d%3 ➔ Not allowed

5	Unary '+' or Unary '-' E.g. +a	Here 'a' cannot be a pointer.	If 'p' is pointer then -p ➔ Not allowed
6	Pre & Post Increment/ Decrement E.g. ++a , b--	Here 'a' must be a pointer or reference to a numeric value.	If 'p' is pointer then p++ ➔ Allowed
7	Assignment '=' or 'op=' E.g. a=b a op= b	Here operands can be of any type except array. Also both operands must be of same type.	If 'str1' and 'str2' are arrays of characters Then str1==str2 ➔Not allowed. It do not compare content of two strings
8	Shift operators '<<' '>>' E.g. a<<b	Here 'a' is shifted by 'b' number of bits; b must be a positive integer.	If 'a' and 'b' are integers then a<<b ➔ Allowed a<<-b ➔ Not allowed

Important Points-:

A) Dynamic Memory Allocation

The dynamic memory allocation functions viz. malloc(), calloc() and free() are declared in <stdlib.h>.

The "sizeof" is an operator and it works at compile time.

When malloc is unable to allocate the requested memory, it returns a null pointer. A null pointer points nowhere.

After calling free(p) the memory pointed by 'p' should not be used. After calling free(p); it is probably the case that 'p' still points at the same memory. However, since we've given the memory back to the system, it's now available for the allocation. One good way to ensure that it's not to be used any more is to set it to a null pointer as given below-:

```
free(p);
p = NULL;
```

B) Command Line Arguments

The minimum count for argc is one; it is when the command line just contained the name of the invoked program with no arguments. The program can find out its own name using the argv[0] string.

If an argument on the command line is to be interpreted as a numerical constant, i' can be converted from a string to integer using functions like atoi(), atol(), atof().

C) Variable Naming Rules in C Language

The variable name cannot be any keyword of C language.

The variable name must begin with either an alphabet or underscore.

The first 32 characters are significant in the variable name.

It is possible that two or more global variables can have same name but we can initialize only one of them.

It is not possible to have two local variables with same name in a scope.

The variable name is case sensitive.

Except underscore there should not be any special character in name of variable even blank space.

† Objective Questions

Que. 8.1) Predicate the output of following program.	**Rough work space.**

`#include<stdio.h>`
`void main()`
`{`
`int i,j;`
`i = printf("Hello");`
`j = printf("\nHello");`
`printf("%d %d", i,j);`
`}`	

A.	5 7
B.	5 6
C.	1 1
D.	Garbage Values

Que. 8.2) Predicate the output of following program.	**Rough work space.**

`#include<stdio.h>`
`int main()`
`{`
`int y=128;`
`const int x=y;`
`printf("%d", ++x);`
`return 0;`
`}`	

A.	Compiler Error
B.	128
C.	129
D.	Run Time Error

Que. 8.3) Predicate the output of following program.

Rough work space

```
#include<stdio.h>
int main()
{
    const int x;
    x=128;
    printf("%d", x);
    return 0;
}
```

A.	128
B.	Garbage Value
C.	Compiler Error
D.	Run Time Error

Que. 8.4) Predicate the output of following program.

Rough work space.

```
#include<stdio.h>                    //Line 1
int main()
{
    const int x=5;
    int *ptrx;
    ptrx = &x;                       //Line 6
    *ptrx = 10;                      // Line 7
    printf("%d\n", x);
    return 0;
}
```

A.	5
B.	10
C.	Compiler Error at Line 7
D.	Compiler Error at Line 6

Que. 8.5) Predicate the output of following program.	**Rough work space.**

```
#include<stdio.h>            //Line 1
int main()
{
    const int x=5;
    const int *ptrx;
     ptrx = &x;              //Line 6
    *ptrx = 10;              // Line 7
    printf("%d", x);
    return 0;
}
```

A.	10
B.	5
C.	Compiler Error at Line 6
D.	Compiler Error at Line 7

Que. 8.6) Predicate the output of following program.	**Rough work space.**

```
#include<stdio.h>                    //Line 1
int main()
{
    int x=5;
    const int *ptrx;
   ptrx = &x;                        //Line 6
   *ptrx = 10;                       // Line 7
    printf("%d\t", x);
    x = 20;                          // Line 9
    printf("%d", x);
    return 0;
}
```

A.	Compiler Error at Line 7 & 9
B.	10 20
C.	Compiler Error at Line 9
D.	Compiler Error at Line 7

Que. 8.7) Predicate the output of following program.	Rough work space.

#include<stdio.h> //Line 1
int main()
{
int x=5;
int* const ptrx;
ptrx = &x; //Line 6
*ptrx = 10; // Line 7
printf("%d", x);
return 0;
}	

A.	5
B.	10
C.	Compiler Error at Line 7
D.	Compiler Error at Line 6

Que. 8.8) Predicate the output of following program.	Rough work space.

#include<stdio.h> //Line 1
int main()
{
int x=5,y=10;
int* const ptrx=&x;
*ptrx = 10; // Line 6
printf("%d", x);
ptrx = &y; //Line 8
*ptrx = 20; // Line 9
printf("%d", y);
return 0;
}	

A.	Compiler Error at Line 8
B.	10
C.	Compiler Error at Line 9
D.	Compiler Error at Line 6

Que. 8.9) Predicate the output of following program.	**Rough work space.**

#include<stdio.h>
int main()
{
    const char *s = "";
    char str[] = "Hello";
    s = str;
    while(*s)
        printf("%c", *s++);
    return 0;
}	

A.	Hello
B.	Runtime Error
C.	Compiler Error
D.	Garbage Value

Que. 8.10) Predicate the output of following program.	**Rough work space.**

#include<stdio.h>
int main()
{
    char* const s = "Bye";
    const char str[] = "Hello";
    s[0]='A'; //Line 6
    s = str; //Line 7
    while(*s)
        printf("%c", *s++); //Line 9
    return 0;
}	

A.	Hello
B.	Aye
C.	Compiler Error at Line 7 & 9
D.	Compiler Error at line 6

Que. 8.11) Predicate the output of following program.	Rough work space.

#include<stdio.h>
int main()
{
    char* const s = "Bye";
    const char str[] = "Hello";
    s[0]='A'; //Line 6
    s = str; //Line 7
    str[0]='A'; //Line 8
    printf("%s %s", s, str); //Line 9
    return 0;
}	

A.	Bye Hello
B.	Aye Aello
C.	Compiler Error at Line 7 & 8
D.	Compiler Error at line 6

Que. 8.12) Predicate the output of following program.	Rough work space.

#include<stdio.h>
int fun(const int t)
{
    t = 10;
    return t;
}
int main()
{
    int a = 5;
    printf("%d", a);
    a= fun(a);
    printf("\t%d", a);
    return 0;
}	

A.	5 5
B.	Compiler Error
C.	5 10
D.	Runtime Error

Que. 8.13) Predicate the output of following program.
#include<stdio.h> //Line 1
int main()
{
char str1[] = "India";
char str2[] = "Great";
char *const ptr = str1; //Line 6
ptr = str2; // Line 7
printf("%s",ptr);
return 0;
}
	Rough work space.

A.	Great
B.	India
C.	Compiler Error at Line 6
D.	Compiler Error at Line 7

Que. 8.14) Predicate the output of following program.
#include<stdio.h>
int main()
{
const int arr[5] = {1, 2, 3, 4, 5};
printf("%d", arr[3]);
arr[3]=10;
printf("\t%d", arr[3]);
return 0;
}
	Rough work space.

A.	4 4
B.	Compiler Error
C.	4 10
D.	4 Garbage Value

Que. 8.15) Predicate the output of following program.	**Rough work space.**

`#include<stdio.h>`
`int fun(int *f)`
`{`
`    *f = 10;`
`    return 0;`
`}`
`int main()`
`{`
`    const int arr[5] = {1, 2, 3, 4, 5};`
`    printf("%d", arr[3]);`
`    fun(&arr[3]);`
`    printf("\t%d", arr[3]);`
`    return 0;`
`}`	

A.	4 4
B.	Compiler Error
C.	4 10
D.	4 Garbage Value

Que. 8.16) Predicate the output of following program.	**Rough work space.**

`#include<stdio.h>`
`int fun(int b[])`
`{`
`    b[3] = 10;`
`    return 0;`
`}`
`int main()`
`{`
`    const int arr[5] = {1, 2, 3, 4, 5};`
`    printf("%d", arr[3]);`
`    fun(arr);`
`    printf("\t%d", arr[3]);`
`    return 0;`
`}`	

A.	4 4
B.	Compiler Error
C.	4 10
D.	4 Garbage Value

Que. 8.17) Predicate the output of following program.
#include<stdio.h>
int fun(const int b[])
{
   b[3] = 10;
   return 0;
}
int main()
{
   const int arr[5] = {1, 2, 3, 4, 5};
   printf("%d", arr[3]);
   fun(arr);
   printf("\t%d", arr[3]);
   return 0;
}
	Rough work space.

A.	4 4
B.	Compiler Error
C.	4 10
D.	4 Garbage Value

Que. 8.18) Predicate the output of following program.
#include<stdio.h>
int main()
{
char str1[]="Hello";
char str2[]="Hello";
char *str3=str1;
if(str1==str2)
{
      printf("Hi");
}
if(str1==str3)
{
      printf("Bye");
}
return(0);
}
	Rough work space.

A.	4 4

B.	Compiler Error
C.	4 10
D.	4 Garbage Value

Que. 8.19) Predicate the output of following program.

Rough work space.

```
#include<stdio.h>
#include<conio.h>
int main()
{
clrscr();
printf("%c","India"[3]);
printf(2+"Hello");
return(0);
}
```

A.	dHello
B.	Compiler Error
C.	Runtime Error
D.	illo

Que. 8.20) Predicate the output of following program.

Rough work space.

```
#include<stdio.h>
int main()
{
char ch='p';
printf("%d  %d",sizeof(ch),sizeof('p'));
return(0);
}
```

A.	1 2
B.	2 2
C.	1 1
D.	Compiler Error

Que. 8.21) Predicate the output of following program.
#include<stdio.h>
int main()
{
int a=1,b=2,c=3,d=4,e;
e=(a*=2)+(b=c=d);
printf("%d",e);
}
	Rough work space.

A.	Compiler Error
B.	2
C.	6
D.	5

Que. 8.22) What will be the output of the program (prog.c) given below if it is executed from the command line?
cmd> prog hi hello bye
/* prog.c */
#include<stdio.h>
int main(int argc, char **argv)
{
printf("Number of arg=%d",argc);
printf("\nProgram Name=%s", argv[0]);
printf("\nProgram Name=%s", *argv);
printf("\nFirst argument=%s", argv[1]);
printf("\nFirst character of program name=%c", **argv);
printf("\nFirst character of first argument=%c", *argv[1]);
return 0;
}
	Rough work space.

Que. 8.23) What will be the output of the program (prog.c) given below if it is executed from the command line?
cmd> prog hi hello bye
/* prog.c */
#include<stdio.h>
#include<stdlib.h>
int main(int argc, char **argv)
{
printf("%s", *++argv);
return 0;
}
	Rough work space.

A.	Compiler Error
B.	Garbage
C.	hello
D.	hi

Que. 8.24) What will be the output of the program (prog.c) given below if it is executed from the command line?
cmd> prog hi hello bye
/* prog.c */
#include<stdio.h>
int main(int argc, char *argv[])
{
int j;
j = argv[1] + argv[2] + argv[3];
printf("%d", j);
return 0;
}
	Rough work space.

A.	Runtime Error
B.	Compiler Error
C.	0
D.	Garbage Value

Que. 8.25) What will be the output of the program (prog.c) given below if it is executed from the command line?	**Rough work space.**

cmd> prog 11 22 33
/* prog.c */
#include<stdio.h>
int main(int argc, char *argv[])
{
int j;
j = atoi(argv[0]) + atoi(argv[1]) + atoi(argv[2]);
printf("%d", j);
return 0;
}	

A.	Runtime Error
B.	Compiler Error
C.	66
D.	33

Que. 8.26) What will be the output of the program (prog.c) given below if it is executed from the command line?	**Rough work space.**

cmd> prog 11 22 33
/* prog.c */
#include<stdio.h>
int main(int argc, char *argv[])
{
int i,j=0;
for(i=1;i<argc;i++)
j = j+atoi(argv[i]);
printf("%d", j);
return 0;
}	

A.	Runtime Error
B.	Compiler Error
C.	Garbage Value
D.	66

Que. 8.27) What will be the output of the program (prog.c) given below if it is executed from the command line?	**Rough work space.**

```
cmd> prog hi hello bye
/* prog.c */
#include<stdio.h>
int main(int argc, char *argv[])
{
    int tcnt=argc;
    while(--tcnt>0)
        printf("%s\t", *++argv);
    while(++tcnt<argc)
        printf("%s\t",*--argv);
    return 0;
}
```

A.	hi hello bye hello hi <prog-name>
B.	hi hello bye hi hello bye
C.	bye hello hi bye hello hi
D.	<prog-name> hi hello bye hi hello bye

Que. 8.28) What will be the output of the program (prog.c) given below if it is executed from the command line?	**Rough work space.**

```
cmd> prog hi hello bye
/* prog.c */
#include<stdio.h>
int main(int argc, char **argv)
{
printf("%s  %d\n", argv[argc],argv[argc]);
    return 0;
}
```

A.	bye Garbage Value
B.	Runtime Error
C.	NULL 0
D.	Compiler Error

Que. 8.29) Which of the following statements are FALSE about the below code?
int main(int ac, char *av[])
{
}
	Rough work space.

A.	The "ac" contains count of arguments supplied at command-line
B.	The "av" contains addresses of arguments supplied at a command line
C.	In place of ac and av, argc and argv should be used.
D.	The variables ac and av are always local to main()

Que. 8.30) Check if following statements are TRUE or FALSE?	
1.	"ARGV" is an array of character pointer.
2.	"ARGV" is a pointer to an array of character pointers.
3.	"ARGV" is an array of strings.
4.	Every time we supply new set of values to the program at command prompt, we need to recompile the program.
5.	Even if integer/float arguments are supplied at command prompt they are treated as strings.
6.	The first argument to be supplied at command-line must always be count of total arguments.

Que. 8.31) Predicate the output of following program ?

Rough work space.

```
#include<stdio.h>
#include<stdlib.h>
int main()
{
    int *p;
    p = (int *)malloc(sizeof(int));
    *p=100;
    free(p);
    printf("%d", *p);
    return 0;
}
```

A.	Garbage Value
B.	Runtime Error
C.	100
D.	Compiler Time Error

Que. 8.32) Predicate the output of following program ?	Rough work space.

#include<stdio.h>
#include<stdlib.h>
int main()
{
int *p;
char *c;
p = (int *)malloc(sizeof(int));
c = (char *)malloc(sizeof(char));
printf("%d %d",
sizeof(p),sizeof(*p));
printf(" %d %d",
sizeof(c),sizeof(*c));
free(p);
free(c);
return 0;
}	

A.	2 2 2 2
B.	1 1 1 1
C.	2 2 2 1
D.	2 2 1 1

Que. 8.33) Predicate the output of following program ?	Rough work space.

#include<stdio.h>
#include<stdlib.h>
int main()
{
int *p;
p = (int *)malloc(260 * 260);
if(p == NULL)
printf("Allocation failed");
else
printf("Allocation Success");
return 0;
}	

A.	Compiler Error
B.	Segmentation fault
C.	Allocation Success
D.	Allocation failed

Que. 8.34) Predicate the output of following program ?	**Rough work space.**

```
#include<stdio.h>
#include<stdlib.h>
int main()
{
    int *a[3];
    a = (int*) malloc(sizeof(int)*3);
//Line 6
    a[0]=10;
//Line 7
    printf("%d",a[0]);
//Line 8
    free(a);
    return 0;
}
```

A.	Garbage
B.	Compiler Error at Line 6
C.	Compiler Error at Line 7
D.	10

Que. 8.35) Predicate the output of following program ?	**Rough work space.**

```
#include<stdio.h>
#include<stdlib.h>
int main()
{
    char *ptr;
    *ptr = (char)malloc(30);
    strcpy(ptr, "RAM");
    printf("%s", ptr);
    ptr[0]='S';
    printf("%s", ptr);
    free(ptr);
    return 0;
}
```

A.	Compiler Error
B.	Runtime Error

C.	RAMSAM
D.	Garbage

Que. 8.36) Predicate the output of following program ?	Rough work space.

```
#include<stdio.h>
int main()
{
        int a[5]={10,1,2,3,4};
        int *p=a;
        int *q=&a[3];
        int r;
        r=q-p;
        printf("\n%d",r);
}
```

A.	Compiler Error
B.	7
C.	-7
D.	3

Que.8.37) Predicate the output of following program ?	Rough work space.

```
#include<stdio.h>
int main()
{
        int a[5]={0,1,2,3,4};
        int *p=a;
        int *q=&a[3];
        int r;
        r=q+p;
        printf("\n%d",r);
}
```

A.	Compiler Error
B.	2
C.	3
D.	6

† Answers with explanations

Answer 8.1	**B. 5 6**
Explanation 8.1	The printf() library function returns number of characters printed on the console. The first call to printf() function prints 5 characters; hence variable 'i' gets the value 5. However in the second call to printf() newline character ('\n') is used which causes value 6 to be assigned to the variable 'j'.

Answer 8.2	**A. Compiler Error**
Explanation 8.2	The variable 'x' is a constant variable; its value cannot be directly modified in the program. Hence "++x" causes the compiler error.

Answer 8.3	**C. Compiler Error**
Explanation 8.3	The variable 'x' is a constant variable; its value cannot be modified in the program. The constant variables need to be initialized at the time of declaration only. Hence "x=128" expressions causes the compiler error.

Answer 8.4	**B. 10**
Explanation 8.4	The variable 'x' is a constant variable. The value of a constant variable cannot be directly modified in the program; however a constant variable can be indirectly modified by a pointer. Hence the expression "*ptrx=10" is a valid expression which causes value 10 for the variable 'x'.

Answer 8.5	D. Compiler Error at Line 7
Explanation 8.5	The variable 'x' is a constant variable. The pointer "ptrx" is declared as a pointer to constant integer. Due to this we cannot modify the value of variable which is pointed by the "ptrx". Hence the expression "*ptrx=10" is not valid expression which causes the compiler error.

Answer 8.6	D. Compiler Error at Line 7
Explanation 8.6	The variable 'x' is a normal variable. The pointer "ptrx" is declared as a pointer to a constant integer. Due to this we cannot modify the value of variable which is pointed by the "ptrx" using the pointer. Hence the expression "*ptrx=10" is not valid expression which causes the compiler error. However the value of variable can be modified using the variable name 'x' as it is a normal variable. Hence "x=20" is a valid expression.

Answer 8.7	D. Compiler Error at Line 6
Explanation 8.7	The pointer "ptrx" is declared as a constant pointer to an integer. Since it is a constant pointer it is necessary to initialize it at the time of declaration itself. Hence the compiler shows error at line 6. There is no error at line 7 as it is possible to change the value of variable which is pointed by "ptrx".

Answer 8.8	A. Compiler Error at Line 8
Explanation 8.8	The pointer "ptrx" is declared as a constant pointer to an integer. The constant pointer once initialized cannot be made to point some other location. Hence the compiler shows error at line 8.

Answer 8.9	A. Hello
Explanation 8.9	The pointer 's' is a pointer to constant character string. Hence the pointer can be made to point another address; but the string content cannot be modified using the pointer 's'. Now consider the expression "*s++"; here '*' and '++' (post-increment) are having same priority and right to left associtivity. Hence printf() prints one character in each iteration of the loop and moves pointer one position ahead due to post increment.

Answer 8.10	C. Compiler Error at Line 7 & 9
Explanation 8.10	The pointer 's' is a constant pointer to a character string. Hence the pointer cannot be made to point another address; but the string content can be modified using the pointer 's'. Hence "s[0]= 'A' " is a valid expression; however expression on line 7 and 9 are not valid as they are trying to change the address in the pointer 's'.

Answer 8.11	C. Compiler Error at Line 7 & 8
Explanation 8.11	The pointer 's' is a constant pointer to a character string. Hence the pointer cannot be made to point another address. Due to this compiler reports an error at line 7. The "str" is a constant array; its content cannot be changed after initialization. Due to this compiler reports an error at line 8.

Answer 8.12	B. Compiler Error
Explanation 8.12	The "fun" accepts a constant integer as argument. The value of constant argument cannot be changed in the function. Hence compiler reports the error due to the expression -: "t=10".

Answer 8.13	**D. Compiler Error at Line 7**
Explanation 8.13	The pointer "ptr" is a constant pointer to a character string. Hence the pointer cannot be made to point another address; but the string content can be modified using the pointer. At line 7 an attempt is made to change the location pointer is pointing to; which is not allowed. Hence the compiler reports error.

Answer 8.14	**B. Compiler Error**
Explanation 8.14	The "arr" is a constant array. The content of constant array cannot be changed in direct way. The statement "arr[3]=10" causes the compiler error.

Answer 8.15	**C . 4 10**
Explanation 8.15	The "arr" is a constant array. The content of constant array can be changed using indirect way (pointer).

Answer 8.16	**C. 4 10**
Explanation 8.16	By default arrays as passed by reference. Here the content of constant array gets changed in the function "fun".

Answer 8.17	**B. Compiler Error**
Explanation 8.17	The compiler reports an error as attempt is made to change the content of constant array in user defined function "fun".

Answer 8.18	D. Bye
Explanation 8.18	The "str1" and "str3" stores address of the same string "Hello". Hence "str1==str3" becomes a TRUE condition. We cannot used "==" operator for string comparisons; rather we should use strcmp() library function for string comparisons. The "str1" and "str2" are pointing to two different addresses; Hence "str1==str2" becomes a FALSE condition.

Answer 8.19	D. illo
Explanation 8.19	The first printf() skips initial three characters and displays the next character i.e. 'i'. The second printf() prints the string after skipping initial two characters i.e. "llo".

Answer 8.20	A. 1 2
Explanation 8.20	The character constant needs 2 bytes of memory space; but a character variable needs only 1 byte of memory space. The 'p' is a character constant. Hence sizeof('p') displays the value 2. The "ch" is a character variable; hence memory allocated for it is one bytes only. Also note that, sizeof() operator in C language find size of a string constant including null character but strlen() function finds number of characters in a string excluding null character.

Answer 8.21	C. 6

Explanation 8.21	The expressions is evaluated as follows -:
	e = (a*=2) + (b=c=4);
	e = (a*=2) + (b=4=4);// value of 'c' becomes 4
	e = (a*=2) + (4=4=4);// value of 'b' becomes 4
	e = (2) + (4=4=4); // value of 'a' becomes 2
	e = 2 + 4 =6

Answer 8.22	Number of arg=4 Program Name=D:\TC\CODES\Q83.EXE Program Name=D:\TC\CODES\Q83.EXE First argument=hi First character of program name=D First character of first argument=h
Explanation 8.22	Please note that when we execute the program from command line then program name is a complete path of the program name e.g. D:\TC\CODES\Q83.EXE. The "argv[0]" is equivalent to "*(argv+0)" or in other way "*argv".

Answer 8.23	**D. hi**
Explanation 8.23	By applying operator precedence and associtivity to the expression "*++argv"; the operator '++' (pre-increment) works first and then '*'. Hence the pointer 'argv' is moved from 0th string to 1st string and displays the string "hi".

Answer 8.24	**B. Compiler Error**
Explanation 8.24	Note that "argv[1]" is a string and not an integer.

Answer 8.25	**D. 33**
Explanation 8.25	The "argv[0]" is program name; it is not string. When atoi function is applied to a string it returns value 0. Hence the sum is 33 (0+11+22).

Answer 8.26	**D. 66**
Explanation 8.26	The program makes addition of arguments supplied at execution time. Following cares are taken to execute the program in correct way-: 1. The string arguments are converted into integers using "atoi". 2. The variable 'j' is initialized to 0. 3. For making addition the arguments taken into consideration are 1st, 2nd and 3rd; 0th argument which is program name is not considered (as it is always a string).

Answer 8.27	**A. hi hello bye hello hi <prog-name>**
Explanation 8.27	Apply operator precedence and associtivity as discussed in previous chapters.

Answer 8.28	**C. NULL 0**
Explanation 8.28	The variable "argc" contains count of number of arguments. Since "argv" is an array it has valid indices from 0 to "argc-1". Hence argv[argc] displays "NULL" irrespective of number of arguments passed to the program. The "%d" displays value 0 which corresponds to "NULL".

Answer 8.29	**C. In place of ac and av, argc and argv should be used.**
Explanation 8.29	The "ac" and "av" are variable names; it is not compulsory to have variable names as argv, argc.

Answer 8.30	**Statement**	**Answer**
1	"ARGV" is an array of character pointer.	True
2	"ARGV" is a pointer to an array of character pointers.	False

3	"ARGV" is an array of strings.	False
4	Every time we supply new set of values to the program at command prompt, we need to recompile the program.	False
5	Even if integer/float arguments are supplied at command prompt they are treated as strings.	True
6	The first argument to be supplied at command-line should be count of total arguments.	False

Answer 8.31	**C. 100**
Explanation 8.31	The call to "free" de-allocate the memory pointed by pointer 'p'; but it is possible that the content of memory exists after the call. Hence the program displays output. 100. Though above program displays the content of variable correctly; it is strongly recommended not to use the variable after de-allocating memory. Otherwise it may lead to unwanted results.

Answer 8.32	**C. 2 2 2 1**
Explanation 8.32	The 'p' and 'c' are pointers; hence they need 2 bytes of storage (on Turbo C). The "*p" is an integer and "*c" is a character; so sizes displayed accordingly.

Answer 8.33	**D. Allocation failed**
Explanation 8.33	Here value 260*260 = 67600 is passed as argument to malloc() function. The memory allocation fails in 16 bit platform (Turbo C in DOS).

Answer 8.34	**B. Compiler Error at Line 6**
Explanation 8.34	On the line number 6 "malloc" function is trying to allocate one chunk of 2*3=6 Bytes rather than allocating memory for array of three integer pointers. Hence it results into the compiler error.

Answer 8.35	**C. RAMSAM**
Explanation 8.35	Here pointer 'ptr' is pointing to a chunk of memory having 30 bytes capacity. The strcpy() function copies the string "RAM" and then first character is changed to 'S'.

Answer 8.36	**D. 3**
Explanation 8.36	The '-'operator can work if two operands are pointers. It displays the number of integers (as pointers to integers are used in this example) in between two addresses.

Answer 8.37	**A. Compiler Error**
Explanation 8.37	The '+'operator cannot work if two operands are pointers.

SUBJECTIVE QUESTIONS

C Language Subjective Question and answers:

Que. 9.1)	Tell about C language?
Ans. 9.1)	The C programming language is developed in the early 1970s by Ken Thompson and Dennis Ritchie for use on the UNIX operating system. It has spread to many other operating systems and is one of the most widely used programming languages. The C language is block structured, and designed for procedural and imperative programming. The C language is very popular for implementing lower or system level software's like compilers, device drivers, operating systems etc.

Que. 9.2)	What is modular programming?
Ans. 9.2)	Modular programming is a programming technique that breaks the program functionality into small modules. Each module has one function that has all codes and variables needed to execute them. Its easy to find out bugs from a very large program in modular programming. The modular programming is also termed as structural programming.

Que. 9.3)	Whether C language is platform dependent or independent?
Ans. 9.3)	The C language is platform dependent. The compliers for C language are different on different platforms. There are several platform dependencies in the C language, such as sizeof(int) and the behavior of arithmetic operators in overflow situations.

Que. 9.4)	What is difference between a declaration and definition?
Ans. 9.4)	A *declaration* provides information that, a function or variable exists and gives the information about data type (in case of a variable) and prototype (in case of a function). The purpose of declarations is to allow the compiler to correctly process references to the declared variables or functions. A *definition* allocates the storage for a variable and initializes it with a value; in case of a function it defines the code of a function.

Que. 9.5)	**What is Header file?**
Ans. 9.5)	The libraries used in C programs consist two parts: 1) A *header file* that define types and macros and declare variables and functions 2) The actual library or *archive* that contains the definitions of the variables and functions. In order to use the facilities in the GNU C library, it is required to include the appropriate header files for successful compilation of the program. Once program has been compiled, the linker resolves the references to the actual definitions provided in the archive file. Actually it is not necessary *to* include a header file to use a function it declares; you can declare the function explicitly in the code according to the specifications in the manual. But it is usually better to include the header file because it may define types and macros that are not otherwise available and because it may define more efficient macro replacements for some functions. It is also a sure way to have the correct declaration.

Que. 9.6)	**What is difference between: #include <stdio.h> and #include "stdio.h"?**
Ans. 9.6)	The above both syntaxes specify a header file for inclusion into the current source program. The difference is where in the directory system the file stdio.h is expected to be. In the case of the brackets (<>), the compiler will look for the file stdio.h in the default location for header files. In the case of the quotes (""), the compiler will only look in the current directory to search the given file.

Que. 9.7)	What are phases in compilation process?
Ans. 9.7)	The compilation process refers to the processing of source code files (.c, .cc, or .cpp) and the creation of an 'object' file. This step doesn't create anything the user can actually run. Instead, the compiler produces the machine language instructions that correspond to the source code file that was compiled. Please note that preprocessor works before the compilation of the program. Following steps are carried out as part of the compilation process. 1 Lexical analysis (*scanning*): In this step the source text is broken into *tokens*. 2 Syntactic analysis (*parsing*): In this step tokens are combined to form syntactic structures which are represented by a *parse tree*. 3 Semantic analysis: In this step intermediate code is generated for each syntactic structure. In this step type checking is also performed. 4 Machine-independent optimization: In this step intermediate code is optimized to improve efficiency. 5 Code generation: In this step intermediate code is translated to relocatable object code for the target machine. 6 Machine-dependent optimization: In this step the machine code is optimized.

Que. 9.8)	What is program linking?
Ans. 9.8)	The Linking refers to the creation of a single executable file from multiple object files. In this step the linker will complain about undefined functions. During the compilation process if the compiler could not find the definition for a particular function, it assumes that the function is defined in some another file. The linker looks into multiple files and tries to find definition of each function which is referenced. The linker is used to change an object code into an executable code by linking together the necessary build in functions.

Que. 9.9)	What are stages from source code to executable?
Ans. 9.9)	Following are the stages to convert a source code to an executable. 1 Compilation: Here source code is converted into re-locatable object codes. 2 Linking: Here many re-locatable binaries are converted into one re-locatable binary. 3 Loading: Here a re-locatable code is converted into absolute binary with all code and data references bound to the addresses occupied in memory. 4 Execution: In execution the control is transferred to the first instruction of the program.

Que. 9.10)	What is an Identifier?
Ans. 9.10)	Identifiers are names which are given to elements of a program such as variables, arrays & functions. Basically identifier is a group of alphabets or digits. Following are the rules for making a valid identifier-: The first character of identifiers must be an alphabet or an underscore. There are no special characters are allowed except the underscore "_". Two underscores are not allowed. Don't use keywords as identifiers.

Que. 9.11)	What are valid keywords in C Language?
Ans. 9.11)	The keywords are reserved and cannot be used as an identifier. Following is the list of valid keyword in C language -: auto double int long break else long switch case enum register typedef char extern return union const float short unsigned continue for signed void default goto sizeof volatile do if static while.

Que. 9.12)	**Discuss basic and derived data types in C.**
Ans. 9.12)	Basic data types available in C language are int, float, char, double etc. The derived data types are those which are constructed by taking help of basic data types. E.g. array, structure, union, pointer.

Que. 9.13)	**Discuss various type qualifiers in C.**
Ans. 9.13)	In C language the variables can have qualifiers in addition to data types. The "const" and "volatile" are two qualifiers available in C language.

Que. 9.14)	**What is a LVALUE and RVALUE?**
Ans. 9.14)	The LVALUE is an expression to which a value can be assigned. The LVALUE expression is located on the left side of an assignment statement, whereas an RVALUE is located on the right side of an assignment statement. Each assignment statement must have a LVALUE and a RVALUE. The LVALUE expression must reference a storable variable in memory; It cannot be a constant. The RVALUE can be a constant or an expression.

Que. 9.15)	**What is a local block?**
Ans. 9.15)	A local block is any portion of a C program that is enclosed by the left brace (*{*) and the right brace (*}*). The variables can be declared within local blocks, but they must be declared only at the beginning of a local block. The variables declared in this manner are visible only within the local block.

Que. 9.16)	**What is a forward reference?**
Ans. 9.16)	A forward reference is a reference to a variable or function before it is defined to the compiler. The cardinal rule of structured languages is that everything must be defined before it is to be used. There are some occasions where this is not possible. E.g. To define two functions in terms of each other.

Que. 9.17)	**Swap two variables without using third variable.**

Ans. 9.17)	Let a=5,b=10;
	1) Process one
	a=b+a;
	b=a-b;
	a=a-b;
	2) Process two
	a=a+b-(b=a);
	3) Process three
	a=a^b;
	b=a^b;
	a=b^a;

Que. 9.18)	**What is the purpose of a function prototype?**
Ans. 9.18)	A function prototype tells the compiler the data types and order of different parameters passed to the function and the data type of the value returned by the function.

Que. 9.19)	**What is a cyclic property of data type in C language?**
Ans. 9.19)	In the data type char ,int,long int if we assign the value beyond range of data type instead of giving compiler error it repeat the same values in cyclic order. E.g. The range of unsigned char is 0 to 255. In this case if we assign a value greater than 255 then value of variable will be changed to a new value using following approach. If number is X where X is greater than 255 then new value = X % 256. If number is Y where Y is less than 0 then new value = 256 – (Y% 256) The similar logic can be applied to other data types.

Que. 9.20)	**What is an argument? Differentiate between formal arguments and actual arguments?**
Ans. 9.20)	The arguments are used to pass the data from calling function to the called function. The arguments available in the function definition are called formal arguments. The arguments used in function call are called as actual arguments.

Que. 9.21)	**What is difference between call by value and call by address?**
Ans. 9.21)	In C language we can pass the parameters to functions using following ways. (a)Call by value In this approach we pass copy of actual variables to a function as a parameter. Hence any modification on parameters inside the function will not reflect in the actual variable. (b) Call by address In this approach we pass memory address of the variables to a function as a parameter. Hence any modification on parameters inside the function will reflect in the actual variable.

Que. 9.22)	**What are the advantages of using unions?**
Ans. 9.22)	The union is a collection of data items of different data types. It can hold data of only one member at a time though it has members of different data types. If a union has two members of different data types, they are allocated the same memory. The memory allocated is equal to maximum size of the members.

Que. 9.23)	**What is automatic type conversion in C language?**
Ans. 9.23)	In C language if two operands are of different data type in a binary operation then before performing any operation compiler will automatically convert the operand of lower data type to higher data type. This concept is known as automatic type conversion.

Que. 9.24)	Whether pointers are integers?
Ans. 9.24)	A pointer is an address not an integer.

Que. 9.25)	What is "void" pointer? What is size of a void pointer?
Ans. 9.25)	The void pointer, also known as the generic pointer, is a special type of pointer that can point object of any data type. Important points about generic pointer are -: 1. We cannot dereference generic pointer. 2. We can find the size of generic pointer using sizeof operator. 3. The generic pointer can hold any type of pointers like char pointer, struct pointer, array of pointer etc. without any typecasting. 4. Any type of pointer can hold generic pointer without any type casting.

Que. 9.26)	What is difference between uninitialized pointer and a null pointer?

Ans. 9.26)	An uninitialized pointer is a pointer which points unknown memory location while null pointer is pointer which points a null value or base address of segment. For example:
	int *p; //Uninitialized pointer
	int *q= (int *)0; //Null pointer

Que. 9.27)	What is dangling pointer in C?
Ans. 9.27)	If a pointer is pointing to the memory address of a variable; and after some time the variable has been deleted from that memory location. In this case the pointer continues to point same memory location; such pointer is known as dangling pointer.

Que. 9.28)	**What is wild pointer in c?**
Ans. 9.28)	A pointer in C which has not been initialized is known as wild pointer. There is difference between the NULL pointer and wild pointer. The NULL pointer points to the base address of segment while wild pointer doesn't point any specific memory location.

Que. 9.29)	**What are merits and demerits of using Arrays?**
Ans. 9.29)	The Arrays have fix size memory allocation. Following are merits of using Arrays: 1) We can easily access each element of array using array indices. 2) The Arrays elements are stored in continuous memory location. Hence all elements are accessible once we have address of the base element. Demerits of using Arrays: (a) Wastage of memory space as we cannot change size of array at the run time. (b) It can store only similar type of data.

Que. 9.30)	**How we can modify the content of constant variable in C?**
Ans. 9.30)	We can modify content of constant variable with the help of pointers.

Que. 9.31)	**What is NULL pointer?**
Ans. 9.31)	The NULL pointer is a pointer which is pointing to nothing. Examples of NULL pointer: 1. int *ptr=(char *)0; 2. float *ptr=(float *)0; 3. char *ptr=(char *)0; 4. double *ptr=(double *)0; 5. char *ptr='\0'; 6. int *ptr=NULL; We cannot copy anything in the NULL pointer. The NULL is macro constant which has been defined in the header file stdio.h as-: #define NULL 0

Que. 9.32)	Which one is faster n++ or n+1?
Ans. 9.32)	The expression n++ requires a single machine instruction. The expression n+1 requires more instructions to carry out this operation. Hence n++ executes faster.

Que. 9.33)	What is the difference between calloc() and malloc()?
Ans. 9.33)	The malloc() and calloc() both are used for dynamic memory allocation in C language. There are two differences between malloc() and calloc() functions: **1.** The malloc() allocates memory in bytes. The programmer specifies how many bytes of memory malloc should allocate and malloc will allocate that many bytes (if possible) and return the address of the newly allocated chunk of memory. E.g. p = (int*) malloc(5*sizeof(int)); The calloc() allocates a chunk of memory specified by a block/element size and the number of blocks/elements. E.g. p = (int*) calloc(5, sizeof(int)); Note that malloc() takes only one argument whereas calloc() accepts two arguments. **2.** The malloc() does not initialize memory after it allocates it. It just returns the pointer back to the calling code and the calling code is responsible for initialization or resetting of the memory. On the other hand calloc() initializes the allocated memory to 0. Due to overhead of memory initialization calloc() is slower than malloc().

Que. 9.34)	What is a memory leak?
Ans. 9.34)	If memory is allocated and it's not released after usage; this results in reducing the available memory for other applications. It causes crashing the application when the computer memory resource limits are reached.

Que. 9.35)	**What is the purpose of realloc( )?**
Ans. 9.35)	Declaration: void *realloc(void **ptr*, size_t *size*); The above function attempts to resize the memory block pointed to by *ptr* that was previously allocated with a call to malloc or calloc. The contents pointed to by *ptr* are unchanged. If the value of *size* is greater than the previous size of the block, then the additional bytes have an un-determinate value. If the value of *size* is less than the previous size of the block, then the difference of bytes at the end of the block are freed. If ptr is null, then it behaves like malloc. If the new space cannot be allocated, then the contents pointed to by *ptr* are unchanged. If size is zero, then the memory block is completely freed. On success a pointer to the memory block is returned (which may be in a different location as before). On failure or if size is zero, a null pointer is returned.

APPENDIX

APPENDIX I :

ASCII Table

Decimal	Hex	Char	Decimal	Hex	Char	Decimal	Hex	Char	Decimal	Hex	Char
0	0	[NULL]	32	20	[SPACE]	64	40	@	96	60	`
1	1	[START OF HEADING]	33	21	!	65	41	A	97	61	a
2	2	[START OF TEXT]	34	22	"	66	42	B	98	62	b
3	3	[END OF TEXT]	35	23	#	67	43	C	99	63	c
4	4	[END OF TRANSMISSION]	36	24	$	68	44	D	100	64	d
5	5	[ENQUIRY]	37	25	%	69	45	E	101	65	e
6	6	[ACKNOWLEDGE]	38	26	&	70	46	F	102	66	f
7	7	[BELL]	39	27	'	71	47	G	103	67	g
8	8	[BACKSPACE]	40	28	(	72	48	H	104	68	h
9	9	[HORIZONTAL TAB]	41	29	)	73	49	I	105	69	i
10	A	[LINE FEED]	42	2A	*	74	4A	J	106	6A	j
11	B	[VERTICAL TAB]	43	2B	+	75	4B	K	107	6B	k
12	C	[FORM FEED]	44	2C	,	76	4C	L	108	6C	l
13	D	[CARRIAGE RETURN]	45	2D	-	77	4D	M	109	6D	m
14	E	[SHIFT OUT]	46	2E	.	78	4E	N	110	6E	n
15	F	[SHIFT IN]	47	2F	/	79	4F	O	111	6F	o
16	10	[DATA LINK ESCAPE]	48	30	0	80	50	P	112	70	p
17	11	[DEVICE CONTROL 1]	49	31	1	81	51	Q	113	71	q
18	12	[DEVICE CONTROL 2]	50	32	2	82	52	R	114	72	r
19	13	[DEVICE CONTROL 3]	51	33	3	83	53	S	115	73	s
20	14	[DEVICE CONTROL 4]	52	34	4	84	54	T	116	74	t
21	15	[NEGATIVE ACKNOWLEDGE]	53	35	5	85	55	U	117	75	u
22	16	[SYNCHRONOUS IDLE]	54	36	6	86	56	V	118	76	v
23	17	[ENG OF TRANS. BLOCK]	55	37	7	87	57	W	119	77	w
24	18	[CANCEL]	56	38	8	88	58	X	120	78	x
25	19	[END OF MEDIUM]	57	39	9	89	59	Y	121	79	y
26	1A	[SUBSTITUTE]	58	3A	:	90	5A	Z	122	7A	z
27	1B	[ESCAPE]	59	3B	;	91	5B	[	123	7B	{
28	1C	[FILE SEPARATOR]	60	3C	<	92	5C	\	124	7C	|
29	1D	[GROUP SEPARATOR]	61	3D	=	93	5D	]	125	7D	}
30	1E	[RECORD SEPARATOR]	62	3E	>	94	5E	^	126	7E	~
31	1F	[UNIT SEPARATOR]	63	3F	?	95	5F	_	127	7F	[DEL]

APPENDIX II :
Operator Precedence & Associativity Table

OPERATORS	ASSOCIATIVITY
( ) [ ] -> .	left to right
! ~ ++ -- + - * & (type) size of	right to left
* / %	left to right
+ -	left to right
<< >>	left to right
< <= > >=	left to right
== ! =	left to right
&	left to right
^	left to right
¦	left to right
&&	left to right
¦ ¦	left to right
? :	right to left
= += - = *= /= %= &= ^= ¦ = <<= >>=	right to left
,	left to right

ISBN	Title	Author	Year	Price

Shroff Reprints & Original Titles
The X Team Series
(An Imprint of Shroff Publishers)

Computers

ISBN	Title	Author	Year	Price
9789350236321	**.NET Interview Q&A, 164 Pages**	**Harwani**	**2012**	**225.00**
9788184041569	Ajax for Beginners (B/CD), 452 Pages	Bayross	2006	375.00
9788184041972	Application Development with Oracle & PHP on Linux for Beginners, 2/ed (B/CD), 940 Pages	Bayross	2007	650.00
9789350233733	Blogging for Beginners, 268 Pages	Harwani	2011	350.00
9788184046397	C for Beginners, 532 Pages	Mothe	2009	350.00
9789350233900	C Interviews Q&A, 192 Pages	Thorat	2011	150.00
9788184046564	C++ for Beginners, 403 Pages	Harwani	2009	375.00
9789350231012	Core Java for Beginners, (B/CD), 892 Pages	Shah	2010	450.00
9788184046694	Database Concepts and Systems for Students, 3/ed, 428 Pages	Bayross	2009	300.00
9788184048780	HTML for Beginners, 2/Ed, 416 Pages	Aibara	2010	350.00
9789350236475	**HTML5 for Beginners, 564 Pages**	**Aibara**	**2012**	**450.00**
9788184047059	Hibernate 3 for Beginners - Covers Java Persistence API (B/CD), 680 Pages	Shah	2009	500.00
9788184045697	Java EE 5 for Beginners, Revised & Enlarged 2/ed (B/CD), 1,192 Pages	Bayross	2008	575.00
9788184049398	Java EE 6 for Beginners, (B/CD), 1092 Pages	Shah	2009	625.00
9788184049411	Java EE 6 Server Programming for Professionals (B/CD), 1,328 Pages	Shah	2010	750.00
9788184048063	Java EE Project using EJB 3, JPA and Struts 2 for Beginners, (B/CD), 1,258 Pages	Shah	2009	750.00
9788184043174	Java for Beginners (B/CD), Covers Java SE 6 JDK, 600 Pages	Chavan	2007	450.00
9788184045932	Java for Professionals: A Practical Approach to Java Programming (Covers Java SE 6), 790 Pages	Harwani	2008	525.00
9789350233719	Java for Students, 2/ed, 850 Pages	Pherwani	2011	600.00
9788184047097	Java Persistence API in EJB 3 for Professionals, (B/CD) 756 Pages	Shah	2009	550.00
9788184045925	JavaServer Pages Project for Beginners, (B/CD), 746 Pgs	Shah	2008	550.00
9788184045598	Java Server Programming for Professionals, Revised & Enlarged 2/ed (Covers Java EE 5) (B/CD), 1,612 Pages	Bayross	2008	700.00
9788184043594	Java Server Pages for Beginners (B/CD), 872 Pages	Bayross	2007	500.00
9788184048438	Lamp Programming for Professionals, (B/CD), 1,284	Shah	2009	800.00
9789350233986	**Mobile Computing for Beginners, 782 Pages**	**Shende**	**2012**	**750.00**
9789350235188	MySQL 5.1 for Professionals (B/CD), 776 Pages	Bayross	2011	650.00
9788184045260	Oracle for Professionals (Covers Oracle 9i, 10g & 11g) (B/CD), 1,420 Pages	Shah	2008	750.00
9788184043228	PC Hardware for Beginners, 308 Pages	Sangia	2007	225.00
9788184040753	PHP 5.1 for Beginners (B/CD), 1,284 Pages	Bayross	2006	650.00

ISBN	Title	Author	Year	Price
9788184048445	PHP Project for Professionals, (B/CD), 1,200 Pages	Shah	2010	750.00
9788184047073	Practical ASP.NET 3.5 Projects for Beginners, (B/CD), 550 Pages	Harwani	2009	425.00
9788184048070	Practical EJB Project for Beginners, 312 Pages	Harwani	2009	325.00
9788184043426	Practical Java Project for Beginners (B/CD), 164 Pages	Harwani	2007	150.00
9788184043419	Practical Web Services for Beginners, 168 Pages	Harwani	2007	150.00
9789350234907	Programming With PL/SQL for Beginners, 236 Pages	Patil	2011	300.00
9788184049725	QuickTest Professional (QTP) Version 10, 116 Pages	Mallepally	2010	125.00
9789350231241	QTP for Professionals, 480 Pages	Reddy	2010	450.00
9788184048100	SAP SD for Beginners, 324 Pages	Samad	2009	350.00
9789350233894	SAP SD for Beginners, 2/ed, 252 Pages	Samad	2011	350.00
9789350236482	**Software Automation Testing Tools for Beginners, 1110 Pgs**	**Shende**	**2012**	**1000.00**
9789350236901	**Spring 3 for Beginners, Pages 612**	**Shah**	**2012**	**575.00**
9788184047448	Struts 2 for Beginners, 2/ed, (B/CD), 566 Pages	Shah	2009	450.00
9788184046960	Struts 2 with Hibernate 3 Project for Beginners, (B/CD), 1,042 Pages	Shah	2009	675.00
9788184041071	Visual Basic 2005 for Beginners (B/CD), 1,172 Pages	Bayross	2006	150.00

Other Computer Titles

ISBN	Title	Author	Year	Price
9789350230237	A Primer on Software Quality Models & Project Management, 640 Pages	Mehta	2010	600.00
9788184044270	Advancements in Information Technology and Information Security, 400 Pages	Gopal	2008	750.00
9788184048827	Art of Creative Destruction: Illustarted Software Testing, Test Automation & Agile Testing, 2/ed, 348 Pages	Puranik	2010	400.00
9788173660030	AS/400 Architecture & Applications, 332 Pages	Lawrence	1993	250.00
9788173660047	AS/400: A Practical Guide to Programming & Operations, 284 Pges	Zeilenga	1993	225.00
9789350232859	Beginning Web Development for Smartphones Developing Web Applications with PHP, MySQL & jQTouch, 252 Pages	Harwani	2011	300.00
9789350231029	C# 4.0 Programming Made Easy, 624 Pages	Kadam	2011	350.00
9789350230244	Computer Architecture and Maintenance, 320 Pages	Kadam	2010	200.00
9788173660016	CICS: A How-To for Cobol Programmers, 428 Pages	Kirk	1993	300.00
9789350235553	**Data Structure and Algorithm, 492 Pages**	**Rukadikar**	**2012**	**400.00**
9788184048957	FAQ's in MFC and MFC Solutions, Vol I (B/CD) 510 Pgs	Naik	2010	350.00
9788173666810	First Encounter with Java Including BlueJ, 386 Pages	Bhutta	2006	225.00
9789350230275	Instant Oracle, 100 Pages	Shah	2010	50.00
9788173664632	Introducing MySQL, 96 Pages	Oak	2005	50.00
9789350230251	Management Information Systems (MIS)	Kadam	2010	150.00
9789350231258	Maximum Oracle with Oracle Best Practices, 772 Pgs	Puranik	2011	500.00
9788173660023	MVS / VSAM for the Application Programmer, 504 Pages	Brown	1993	325.00
9788184047899	Operating Systems, 2/ed, 408 Pages	Sumitradevi	2009	300.00
9789350236918	**Oracle Financials 11i: A Practical Guide for the Beginners, 2nd Edition, 436 Pgs**	**Peri**	**2012**	**725.00**
9788173668012	Software Defect Prevention Concepts and Implementation, 180 Pages (H/B)	Kane & Bajaj	2003	300.00
9789350236307	**Software Testing: Interview Questions, 176 Pages**	**Reddy**	**2012**	**175.00**

ISBN	Title	Author	Year	Price
9789350230237	Software Quality Models & Project Management in a Nutshell, 640 Pages	Mehta	2010	600.00
9788173668814	Strategic Bidding: A Successful Approach, 192 Pgs	Garg	2004	250.00
9788173660078	TCP/IP Companion: A Guide for the Common User, 284 Pgs	Arick	1993	225.00
9789350231005	Testing in 30+ Open Source Tools, (B/CD), 1080 Pages	Shende	2010	675.00
9788173660429	Vijay Mukhi's ERP Odyssey: Implementing. People Soft Financials 7.0/7.5, 528 Pages	Mukhi	1999	350.00

Business, Management & Finance

ISBN	Title	Author	Year	Price
9788184046977	An Introduction to Foreign Exchange & Financial Risk Management, (B/CD), 348 Pages	Lakshman	2009	400.00
9789350230268	Bootstrapping A Software Company, 348 Pages	Yadav	2010	425.00
9788184044287	Breaking the Black Box, (B/CD), 276 Pages	Pring	2008	500.00
9789350230220	Complete Guide to Technical Analysis: An Indian Perspective, 612 Pages	Pring	2010	500.00
9788184040425	Developing Analytical Skills: Case Studies in Management, 636 Pages	Dr. Natarajan	2008	500.00
9788173660993	Doing Business with the French, 150 Pages	Jhangiani	1999	150.00
9788184044744	Ethics, Indian Ethos and Management, 252 Pages	Balachandran	2008	175.00
9789350231227	Financial Decision Modeling Operations Research & Business Statistics, 696 Pages	Sridhar	2010	350.00
9789350230794	Financial Management: Problems & Solutions, 4/ed, 1,228 Pages	Sridhar	2010	600.00
9788184045611	Futures & Options: Equities & Commodities, 3/ed, 410 Pgs	Sridhar	2008	450.00
9789350232965	Futures & Options, 4th Edition, 392 Pages	Sridhar	2011	450.00
9789350233917	Globally Distributed Work: Concepts, Strategies & Models, 276 Pages	Jain	2011	425.00
9789350233887	Hospitality Management, 476 Pages	Shirke	2011	525.00
9788184040432	How to Eat The Elephant? The CEO's Guide To An Enterprise Sys Implementation, 104 Pages	Tulsyan	2007	325.00
9789350230459	How to Learn Management from your wife, 96 Pgs	Rangnekar	2010	125.00
9789350233108	How to Learn Management from your wife (HB), 96 Pgs	Rangnekar	2010	275.00
9788184044447	How to Select Stocks Using Technical Analysis, (B/CD), 338 Pages	Pring	2008	500.00
9788184044164	Logistics in International Business, 2/ed, 428 Pages	Aserkar	2007	450.00
9788184047547	Magic and Logic of Elliott Waves, The, 204 Pages	Kale	2009	500.00
9788184048568	Management Accounting & Financial Analysis for C.A.Final (June 2009), 9/ed, 540 Pages	Sridhar	2009	400.00
9789350235126	Management of Services, 348 Pages	Poddar	2011	450.00
9788184044454	Momentum Explained, Volume I (B/CD), 366 Pages	Pring	2008	600.00
9788184044461	Momentum Explained, Volume II (B/CD), 338 Pages	Pring	2008	550.00
9788184047066	Purchasing and Inventory Management, 338 Pages	Menon	2009	375.00
9789350233870	Quantitative Techniques for Project Management, 268 Pgs	Velayoudam	2011	600.00
9788173666797	Rules of Origin in International Trade, 238 Pages	Dr. Sathpathy	2005	300.00

ISBN	Title	Author	Year	Price
9789350233580	Services Marketing, 448 Pages	Balachandran	2011	425.00
9789350233115	Soft Skills In Management, 148 Pages	Rangnekar	2011	125.00
9789350235560	Strategic Financial Management for C.A. Final, 7/ed 924 Pages	Sridhar	2011	650.00
9788173668814	Strategic Bidding: A Successful Approach, 192 Pages	Garg	2004	250.00
9788184043211	Time Your Trades With Technical Analysis (B/CD), 348 Pages	Pradhan	2007	600.00

Catering & Hotel Management

ISBN	Title	Author	Year	Price
9788173668739	Careers in Hospitality - Hotel Management Entrance Exam Guide, 332 Pages	Rego	2004	200.00
9789350233887	Hospitality Management, 476 Pages	Shirke	2011	525.00
9789350230817	Marvels of Indian Snacks, 264 Pages	Shankaran	2011	350.00
9788184044751	Marvels of South Indian Cuisine, 220 Pages	Shankaran	2008	250.00
9788184046687	Marvels of North Indian Cuisine, 196 Pages	Shankaran	2009	250.00

Civil Engineering

ISBN	Title	Author	Year	Price
9789350233252	Concrete for High Performance Sustainable Infrastructure, 312 Pages	Newlands	2011	750.00
9789350233245	New Developments in Concrete Construction, 296 Pgs	Dhir	2011	750.00
9788184048056	Raina's Concrete Bridge Practice: Construction, Maintenance & Rehabiliation 2/ed, 452 Pgs (H/B) [14 Colour]	Dr. Raina	2010	600.00
9788184048049	Raina's Concrete Bridge: Inspection, Repair, Strengthening, Testing, Load Capacity Evaluation 2/ed, 800 Pages (H/B) [32 Full Color Inserts]	Dr. Raina	2010	1,200.00
9788184047530	Raina's Concrete for Construction: Facts and Practice, 400 Pages (H/B)	Dr. Raina	2009	650.00
9788184047875	Raina's Construction & Contract Management, 2/ed Inside Story, 585 Pages (H/B)	Dr. Raina	2009	750.00
9788184043785	Raina's Concrete Bridge Practice, 3/ed : Analysis, Design & Economics, 856 Pages (H/B)	Dr. Raina	2007	1,000.00
9788184046618	Raina's Field Manual for Highway and Bridge Engineers, 3/ed,1,404 Pages (H/B)	Dr. Raina	2009	1,800.00
9788184040135	The World of Bridges, 300 Pages (H/B) [4 color]	Dr. Raina	2006	500.00
9789350231180	Using Primavera 6: Planning, Executing, Monitoring and Controlling Projects, 228 Pages	Al-Saridi	2010	275.00
9788184043167	Using Primavera Project Planner Version 3.1 Courseware, 256 Pages	Hamad	2010	300.00
9788184047042	Using STAAD Pro 2007: Courseware with American Design Codes, 356 Pages	Hamad	2009	375.00

Chartered Accountancy

ISBN	Title	Author	Year	Price
9789350231227	Financial Decision Modeling Operations Research & Business Statistics, 696 Pages	Sridhar	2010	350.00

ISBN	Title	Author	Year	Price
9789350232965	Futures & Options: Equities - Trading Strategies & Skills, 392 Pages	Sridhar	2011	450.00
9788184048568	Management Accounting & Financial Analysis for C.A.Final (June 2009), 9/ed, 540 Pages	Sridhar	2009	400.00
9789350235560	Strategic Financial Management for C.A. Final, 7/ed 924 Pages	Sridhar	2011	650.00

Communication

ISBN	Title	Author	Year	Price
9789350231265	Knowing Your Word's Worth: A Practical Guide to Communicating Effectively in English, 180 Pages	Shirodkar	2011	175.00

Dental / Health / Medical

ISBN	Title	Author	Year	Price
9788173669798	The Balancing Act "A Win Over Obesity", 296 Pages	Dr. Gadkari	2005	225.00
9788184049480	The Balancing Act "Know Your Heart", 368 Pages	Dr. Gadkari	2010	250.00
9788173668975	Splinting Management of Mobile & Migrating Teeth, 104 Pages	Dr. Kakar	2004	150.00

Economics

ISBN	Title	Author	Year	Price
9788184043266	Analysing Macroeconomics: A Toolkit for Managers, Executives & Students (H/B), 156 Pages	Rakesh Singh	2007	500.00
9788184044171	Analysing Macroeconomics: A Toolkit for Managers, Executives & Students (P/B), 156 Pages	Rakesh Singh	2007	250.00

Electrical Engineering

ISBN	Title	Author	Year	Price
9788184043235	Basic Electrical Circuits, 2/ed, 368 Pages	Dr. Salam	2007	250.00

Electronics & Communication

ISBN	Title	Author	Year	Price
9788173669002	Electronic Components and Materials, 3/ed, 404 Pages	Joshi	2004	175.00

Electronics & Engineering

ISBN	Title	Author	Year	Price
9788173663772	Principles of Environmental Science Engineering and Maintenance, 288 Pages	Dr. Thirumurthy	2004	175.00

Event Management

ISBN	Title	Author	Year	Price
9788184044959	Enabling Event-ful Experiences, 250 Pages	Balachandran	2008	250.00

General Titles

ISBN	Title	Author	Year	Price
9788184045642	Hello Police Station (Marathi), 118 Pages	Shinde	2008	100.00
9789350231760	Mom Don't Spoil Me, 140 Pages	Dr. Mishra	2010	150.00

HRD

ISBN	Title	Author	Year	Price
9788184047080	Departmental Enquiries: Concept, Procedure & Practice, 534 Pages	Goel	2009	475.00
9788184046229	How To Improve Trainer Effectiveness, 170 Pages	Balachandran	2008	200.00

ISBN	Title	Author	Year	Price

Law

ISBN	Title	Author	Year	Price
9789350230800	A Handbook on the Maintenance & Welfare of Parents & Senior Citizens Act, 2007., 160 Pages	Gracias	2010	150.00
9788173664151	Customs Valuation in India 3/ed, 262 Pages	Satapathy	2002	375.00
9788184042481	Laws of Carriage of Goods By Sea & Multimodal Transport In India, 92 Pages	Hariharan	2007	60.00
9788173661426	Law of Sale of Goods & Partnership, 228 Pages	Chandiramani	2000	150.00
9789350231289	Social Security, Insurance & The Law, 460 Pgs	Gopalakrishna	2011	600.00

Learning Disability

ISBN	Title	Author	Year	Price
9789350233924	On the wave of Brain: A Broad Perspective of Learning Disability 300 Pages	Jain	2011	450.00

Marine

ISBN	Title	Author	Year	Price
9788184043242	Containerisation, Multimodal Transport and Infrastructure Development in India, 5/ed, 852 Pages	Hariharan	2007	650.00
9788173660375	M.S. (STCW) Rules, 1998 incl. Training & Assessment Programme - 1,216 Pages	DG Shipping	1998	225.00
9788173661419	Maritime Education, Training & Assessment Manual (TAP) - Vol II, 474 Pages,	DG Shipping	1999	400.00
9788184043136	Marine Control Technology, 336 Pages	Majumder	2007	400.00
9788173669279	Marine Diesel Engines, 428 Pages	Aranha	2004	250.00
9788184048544	Marine Electrical Technology, 5/ed, 1,250 Pages	Fernandes	2010	750.00
9788173660801	Marine Internal Combustion Engines, 272 Pages	Kane	2003	150.00
9788173660146	Safety Management Systems: An Underconstruction Activity, 98 Pages	Singhal	1998	95.00
9788173665516	A Textbook on Container & Multimodal Transport Management, 522 Pages	Dr. Hariharan	2002	500.00

Motivation

ISBN	Title	Author	Year	Price
9788184044249	Break Your Negative Attitude, 114 Pages	Dr. Mishra	2007	125.00
9788173665271	Heads You Win, Tails You Win, 2/ed, 200 Pages	Dr. Mishra	2005	200.00
9789350236208	**Life is Fundamentally Management!, 200 Pages**	**Senthival**	**2012**	**250.00**
9789350230206	Nothing Is Absolute, 274 Pages	Balachandran	2010	300.00

Parenting

ISBN	Title	Author	Year	Price
9789350231760	Mom Don't Spoil Me, 140 Pages	Dr. Mishra	2010	150.00

Patent

ISBN	Title	Author	Year	Price
9788184047882	Breeding Innovation & Intellectual Capital, 2/ed, 196 Pgs	Dr. Batra	2009	600.00

Physics

ISBN	Title	Author	Year	Price
9788184043259	Gravitation Demythicised: An Introduction to Einstein's General Relativity and Cosmology for Common Man, 258 Pages	Shenoy	2007	250.00

ISBN	Title	Author	Year	Price
9788184047929	Study Aid Theoretical Physics - Volume I: Relativistic Theory and Electrodynamics, 418 Pages	Prof Fai	2010	300.00
9788184047912	Theoretical Physics - Volume I: Relativistic Theory and Electrodynamics, 490 Pages	Prof Fai	2010	400.00

Project Management

ISBN	Title	Author	Year	Price
9789350230237	A Primer on Software Quality Models & Project Management, 640 Pages	Mehta	2010	600.00
9788184048568	Management Accounting & Financial Analysis for C.A.Final (June 2009), 9/ed, 540 Pages	Sridhar	2009	400.00
9789350233870	Quantitative Techniques for Project Management, 268 Pages	Velayoudam	2011	600.00

Self-Help

ISBN	Title	Author	Year	Price
9788184047905	Enhancing Soft Skills, 346 Pages	Biswas	2009	375.00

- **All Prices are in Indian Rupees**
- **Titles Released after January 2012 are marked in Bold.**